# TEACHER
# TOP 5

*Nationally Recognized Teachers Share*
*Their Top 5 Strategies for Successful Teaching*

## T. Nick Ip

www.teachertop5.com

Teacher Top 5™

First Edition, 2013
Printed in the United States of America
ISBN 978-1-61927-646-8
Book cover design by Amber Watson
Author Photograph by Andrew Zinn of Zinn Photography

www.teachertop5.com

*Dedicated to all the amazing educators who make learning come alive in the classroom.*

# CONTENTS

*Secondary Education*

# ACKNOWLEDGEMENTS

While I was afforded the privilege of interviewing many amazing educators, only 25 were included in the *Teacher Top 5* print version. All interviewees, however, were inspirational and publisher-worthy. With deepest gratitude, I thank you for everyone's time, thoughtfulness, and understanding.

Thank you to Kim, my wife and über-supporter, and Otto, my accompanying co-pilot through this wonderful journey of learning and enlightenment.

Thanks also to all the amazing students that I have had the privilege to teach. You have inspired me in countless ways, bringing the magic of teaching and poetry into my life. Your kindness and laughter will always be remembered and cherished.

# INTRODUCTION

## Why Teacher Top 5?

When I first started teaching, I struggled mightily like most teachers do. During my student teaching year in New York City, I remember specifically having difficulty with a student who was not only apathetic about school, but also acted out with behavioral problems. He couldn't care less about learning and was headed down a bad path. As many times as I worked with him, the principal met with him, or his mother received phone calls from my supervising teacher, nothing seemed to change his attitude. I was perplexed about how to help and it troubled me.

Fast-forward several years later and I am in my own classroom in Los Angeles. To my delight, my students are thriving, love to learn, and adore school. Even though I know there is much more I need to learn as a teacher, I feel pretty confident. That said, I think back to that student in New York. What's the difference between him and the students who currently exist in my class? They're all about the same age. They all have similar interests of sports and music. What is it?

Upon deep reflection, I concluded that the single biggest difference between that child in New York and my students in Los Angeles is that no one had a really strong connection with him. Not me (his student teacher), my master teacher, the principal, even his mother, or anyone else.

In my own classroom in Los Angeles, I was there for my students every day. I was even available to them before and after school. I always had students booked for lunch several months in advance on my calendar. I knew all of my students like the back of my hand. What did each student like? What did they dislike? What was his or her family background? What inspired each one? You name it, I knew it.

As I grew as a teacher, I thought back to that student in New York City. How could his experience at school have been better? What would have changed him? What was missing? It took me a while, but I believe the answer is that a strong and close relationship between student and teacher was absent. Without that, it was nearly impossible to reach, connect, and allow him to see that we cared.

This relationship building between teacher and student is vital and perhaps the most important strategy that I use in my own teaching. Yet, no person or educational book ever shared that teaching strategy explicitly. Instead, I was left to my own devices.

When I became a curriculum coordinator at my school, I had the idea of creating a venue whereby teachers could share their best teaching practices. What could I learn from other teachers? Prior to that, I discovered that some teachers coveted their finest trade secrets and maintained a certain level of educational proprietorship. While it is somewhat understandable – teachers spend an inordinate amount of time to perfect their craft – I believe that to be destructive. As educators, we are all in the same boat, striving to improve our teaching for the greater good of future generations. That is why I advocated for a forum to share best practices. The intent was to accelerate the effectiveness of classroom teaching in a collaborative manner. By doing so, each teacher could ascend the learning curve quickly without having to figure things out simply on his or her own.

The result was "Teacher Top 5."

In a direct manner, teachers were asked, "What are the top 5 teaching strategies you utilize to make your teaching effective?" The "Teacher Top 5" platform was developed so that every teacher, no matter how new or seasoned, shared their best-of-breed teaching strategies. After all, we can learn from each other. This forum for knowledge-sharing ended up as a big success, promoting an exchange of ideas and opening up a dialogue for genuine collaboration.

The *Teacher Top 5* book piggybacks off of this initial idea of collaborative learning. It enlightens readers about how stellar teaching is accomplished, what it looks and feels like in the classroom, and how it affects each child. Best yet, teaching strategies are provided by highly distinguished teachers. All of the contributing educators have real, front line, classroom experience. Most importantly, all of them are outstanding. Individuals include State and National Teachers of the Year, professors, and up-and-coming teachers.

In addition, *Teacher Top 5* profiles the exceptional teachers. Who are these educators who have decided to give of themselves to serve others, knowing that the monetary rewards are meager and social status is modest? What compelled them to seek a higher calling?

What makes them so great?

Perhaps it is the story of a young boy who was diagnosed with Tourette Syndrome and learning difficulties, but eventually grew up to become a Fulbright Scholar and a State Teacher of the Year. Maybe it is the arduous journey of a Vietnamese refugee who was airlifted from the ocean to escape war, but excelled in the United States, ultimately graduating magna cum laude from college and honored as a State Teacher of the Year. Then again, possibly it is the biography of a young girl who lost her parents in her formative years, experienced financial hardship, served as a United States Marine in the Gulf War, graduated from college thereafter, and subsequently became an outstanding and empathetic teacher who was recognized as her State's Teacher of the Year.

All of the teachers profiled have a compelling history that allows them to understand how best to connect with students and teach different types of learners. For that reason, *Teacher Top 5* serves as a professional learning community where we can all learn from and about each other. In my own journey in teaching, I truly wished that there existed a single resource for best teaching practices from some of the most esteemed educators. That way, I might have been able to reach that student in New York City. Moreover, it would have made my daily teaching life a lot richer without having to learn simply on my own.

To build a true community of learning and collaboration, won't you join us in sharing your "Teacher Top 5?" Please go to www.teachertop5.com.

# PRIMARY EDUCATION

# CHAPTER 1

**Joseph Masiello**
Delaware State Teacher of the Year (2011)
(English – Grade 6)

*"A teacher affects eternity [the future]; he can never tell where his influence stops."*

— *Henry Adams*

When Henry Adams wrote this quote in his book, *The Education of Henry Adams,* he recognized the awesome power teachers have in shaping the future. Joseph Masiello subscribes to that belief and works hard each day to make sure that power and influence are conducted in the most responsible manner possible. Joe states, "Teaching is a profession that you can wake up each day and have the power to change the world." As a teacher, Joe always keeps Adams' quote in mind. Every interaction between teacher and student can be positive or negative, and affect a child on a going forward basis.

Joe recounts a memory back in sixth grade. Even though he was not a strong academic student, he loved to dance. One day in the cafeteria, he was dancing with a number of girls and having a good time. A teacher observed this, approached, and told him to "sit down and stop acting like a girl." Joe shares that he sat down and never danced again.

Upon reflection and as a teacher, Joe wonders, "What outcome would have resulted if that teacher chose a different approach?" Did that teacher comprehend his power of influence upon a young person? Recognizing this, Joe has made a point to conduct himself in way that encourages kids to be who they are as opposed to bringing them down. It is the teacher's responsibility to create a nurturing and caring environment where all students are accepted for who they are, rather than who the teacher wants them to be.

## Background

Joseph Masiello has had his fair share of good and bad teachers. As a child, Joe was diagnosed with Tourette's Syndrome and was hyperactive. Joe shares that it was probably attention-deficit hyperactivity disorder, but little was known about his condition at that time. He spent his formative years in special education classes and demonstrated difficulty with reading.

In third grade, Joe remembers the reading ability groups set forth with tracking. There were four groups: robins (high), blue jays (medium), cardinals (low); there was a fourth group that was "pulled out," whereby students were taken out of the general classroom setting for specialized instruction. The last group was known as the "bird poop" group by students. Joe was part of the "bird poop" group. While other students may have frowned upon this latter group, Joe had no idea. Instead, Mrs. Brabson, his special education teacher, made him feel like he was talented and gifted. He believed that was why he was pulled out. She worked hard to help him overcome his reading challenges. She built him up to be proud of who he was. When Joe would return to his class after a session, he was confident, content, and felt that he was special. Joe professes, "Mrs. Brabson is my hero. She knew how to teach and reach every child."

For the past 30 years, Joe has made it his priority to reach all kinds of learners and accept each for who he or she is. At the Cab Calloway School of Arts, he teaches sixth grade English and absolutely loves it. As a result of his passion in educating youth, Joe was named the 2011 Delaware Teacher of the Year. He also received an Honorary Degree from the Cab Calloway School of the Arts.

Joe is a graduate from the University of Delaware with a bachelor's degree in education. He is also a two-time Fulbright Scholarship winner.

**Teacher Top 5**

1. _Always Be 100% Prepared When Students Arrive in the Classroom_: One of the central tenets for successful teaching is making certain that everything is prepared and set to go. Joe asserts, "Everything is on the board. Everything is setup. I'm not finishing up. I'm not grading papers. Teachers should be completely ready. Teachers are there for them [students]." Even before instruction begins, he can answer

questions, build rapport, and observe student dynamics. This fosters a sense of confidence from teacher to student and creates a culture of strong competence. Joe states, "When students arrive in my classroom, I'm 100% theirs." For teachers who have difficulty with this, Joe suggests, "Get to school early." Teaching is an awesome responsibility and students should not be treated less than they deserve.

2. _Leave Your Ego at the Door and Take Nothing Personally_: Joe believes that the classroom can often become a microcosm when teachers spend their entire day with children. For that reason, there is a tendency for teachers to feel that it is about them. Joe insists, "Teaching is about the children and has nothing to do with me." As an example, Joe remembers a lesson that he taught a while back. First, he prepared the lesson extensively. Then, he taught it. When he was finished, Joe loved it, but the students did not. The lesson simply did not translate well. Instead of being upset and taking it personally, Joe self-reflected and tried to understand why his lesson flopped so he could make it better next time. That can only be done when one's ego is left at the door.

Whether students are 10 or 17 years old, teachers must also remember that students are children. Sometimes, student behavior may test the patience of the most even-tempered educator. Therefore, it is somewhat common to hear a teacher say, "I hate/dislike that kid." Joe recommends taking a step back and keeping in mind that these are kids, young people. In fact, they are the reason why you are there. As the adult in the classroom, nothing should be taken so personally to compel "you [to] hate a child or dislike them." He proposes, "If you remove your ego, students can't rattle you to 'hate.'" He adds, "Remember, teaching is about the children, not about the teacher."

3. _Be Flexible with Your Employee Contract When It Involves Students and After-School Commitments_: Teachers are in a unique position to affect change in people's lives. So, when it comes to employee contracts, after-school meetings, and labor disputes, Joe always asks, "Is the choice better for you or the kids?" Every time the question arises, he chooses what is best for his students and wishes all teachers would do the same.

Many years ago at his school, the teacher's union picketed for increased salaries. As a union member, Joe agreed to participate, considering it was done before school started. When the union decided that teachers would "work to the letter – e.g., teachers must leave after school once students leave," Joe balked. At that point, it was hurting the kids, especially the ones who needed additional help after school. Joe argues, "It is impossible to give 100% to your students, while abiding to each and every article of your teaching contract." Hence, flexibility is imperative. This runs along the same lines when the principal calls for an important after school meeting. While teachers are technically not obligated to remain after school, as stated in their contract, Joe deems inflexibility as a disservice to the true meaning of education.

4. _Begin Each Day with a Prayer of Thanks_: As a spiritual person, Joe conducts a small personal ritual in the morning prior to the arrival of students. He performs a short breathing exercise to clear his mind. Thereafter, he says a quick prayer stating, "Let me be able to do what I know is right. Help me keep my ego out of the day so that I make good decisions that will benefit my students." Joe does all of this, because he believes that teaching children is a blessing and it should be treated as such. Like his chosen quote from Henry Adams, Joe

reiterates, "Teaching is one of the few jobs that allows you a new opportunity each day to change the world. I begin each day with a silent prayer for guidance. It's a big responsibility."

5. *Make an Effort to Empower Students Each Day*: Educators have an amazing opportunity to change the lives of children. Therefore, Joe asserts, "Make sure you go through life not asleep, but be wide awake. Find ways to empower your students."

As an example, Joe recounts an experience, teaching twelfth grade creative writing. In his class, there was a young girl who was originally from Puerto Rico. She was a modest writer and seemed disconnected from school. When Joe would teach, he would occasionally praise students publicly to recognize their writing effort. One specific time, Joe complimented the young girl. He shared that the student really understood the assignment and turned in a paper filled with pathos for her home country of Puerto Rico. While the paper was not the best written, Joe announced, "It made him feel like he was there." When this student realized that Joe was commending her writing, she was completely surprised. Fast-forward six months, this same girl approached Joe one day. She confided that she had always hated school and did not know how long she could endure it. All that changed, however, due to Joe's class. Nowadays, she claims that school was much easier and she looks forward to each day. The moral of the story, according to Joe, is that it was so easy to empower a student. He states, "It cost me nothing, but it gave her so very much."

**Other Interview Questions**
*1. Who is/are your role model(s) from an educational perspective?*

There are several individuals who Joe identifies as his heroes. The most obvious one is Mrs. Betty Brabson, his third grade special education teacher. One of her most outstanding qualities was her ability to make kids feel good about themselves. Joe asserts, "She was kind and believed in us." After winning the State Teacher of the Year Award, Joe reconnected with Mrs. Brabson to thank her for everything she did. He declares, "If she doesn't constitute a hero or someone to look up to, I don't know who does."

Joe also considers his parents his heroes. His parents, who are not teachers, understood how to reach different types of learners. As a child, Joe remembers how his parents invented ways to help him with his studies. For instance, they applied mnemonics for spelling. In fact, Joe learned the periodic table of elements via limericks. They made learning relevant to their son, making it real with identifiable connections. To date, Joe adopts this same philosophy for his own teaching, facilitating learning by making it relevant.

Moreover, Joe thinks of Oprah Winfrey as a hero. She is a highly public role model who Joe believes deserves a lot of credit. Joe proclaims, "She gives back to children and always supports teachers."

*2. When you take a look at teachers, in general, and recognize all the hard work and devotion they put into their jobs, what would you say is the one thing that you think teachers can improve upon so they can become more highly effective?*

First and foremost, Joe believes that teachers must stay current and know what's going on in the world. This is as basic as knowing what television shows students are watching on MTV. After all, this is the competition vying for students' attention. Keeping informed also pertains to pedagogy and technology. As one of the more senior teachers at his school, Joe confides, "Don't be afraid of technology. You have to be willing to say, 'I don't know what I'm doing.'" Then, reach out to colleagues, and even students, for help and assistance. The days of expecting students to come to class, read quietly, and be fully engaged are unrealistic. Joe believes that there are so many other distractions, including social issues, extracurricular activities, and personal interests. While being an entertainer is not necessary, educators must be relevant and able to keep their students on task.

*3. Are there policies that your school (or past school) has adopted which allow teachers to excel?*

Teaching at a creative arts school allows for enormous pedagogical flexibility. Even though the curriculum is the same as any other public school, Joe has the latitude to integrate arts in his delivery of instruction. Joe believes that this is an enormous advantage, because children naturally gravitate to the arts whether it is performing, singing, dancing, or otherwise. "I love it!" announces Joe. "I can teach through song and dance. I even have a closet full of wigs." While singing and dancing may not be for everyone, Joe suggests teaching through one's passion and sharing it with the students. He states, "For example, if you love race cars, come dressed as a race car driver one day. They'll [the students] love it!" From there, the opportunity to connect and reach your students is much greater as compared to a generic classroom where students know nothing about their teacher.

*4. In order to improve our educational system, what are the shortcomings you notice in schools? What are some of the good things happening? What do you think needs to change?*

School funding and the status of the teaching profession are two areas that need attention. Joe is concerned that all schools are not funded equally, especially if a school is located in an impoverished area. "When it comes to children, funding should be equal," states Joe. "This means the same books and pencils." The disparity is very distinct and must be addressed.

Along the same lines, Joe feels that the teaching profession suffers from a lack of societal respect and is perceived as a "lesser" profession. Back in 2006, Joe won the Fulbright Cultural Exchange Award and he was afforded the opportunity to teach and explore Japan's educational system for two months. In Asia, teachers are revered and looked upon with the utmost dignity. This is considerably different compared to the United States. In America, Joe believes that the salary level of a specific occupation determines much of how a profession is regarded. Sadly, teaching is not a high paying job. Therefore, its recognition is minimized. Joe concludes that teaching salaries should be higher. However, he postulates that the low salary acts as a gatekeeper to assure that individuals who enter the profession do so, not because of the money, but because they want to make a difference.

# CHAPTER 2

## Joy Weiss
Arizona State Teacher of the Year (2010)
(Elementary – Grades 1 and 3)

*"Education is not preparation for life; education is life itself!"*

— *John Dewey*

Over the years, the great John Dewey has inspired countless educators. Joy Weiss is one of them. She shares that Dewey's quote has been her mantra for dozens of years. Joy states, "In the public eye, there is this idea that education is something you do when you go to school. I grew up with a totally different idea. Education is what takes place in every setting and in any situation…it's not just being in the classroom."

Education is not static. It is not based on a specific time or place. Most of all, it should not be seen as only occurring in an academic environment. "It's not just preparing us for life. It is life. We constantly learn. We constantly evolve. We constantly grow," says Joy. She continues, "And, if we didn't, then we wouldn't be where we are today as a society, as a people, or anything else." So in all, Dewey was right when he equated education with life. It happens all around us and that's what Joy believes.

## Background

Joy Weiss is a teacher. She has always been, and will always be. Joy asserts, "I was born to teach." Ever since kindergarten, Joy wanted to be a school teacher. Much of it has to do with her family background. Like many young people with challenging family dynamics, school was her only safe haven, providing security and stability. Joy's father was an alcoholic and her mother suffered from bipolar disease. The volatile nature of family life was only steadied by her warm-hearted, kindergarten teacher, Mrs. Virginia Walker. Joy shares, "Every day, I went to school with baggage. But when I got to school, I knew I was safe." In her kindergarten classroom, she thrived. When it was time for dismissal, Mrs. Walker brought Joy home. Joy adds, "I would stay with her, and she brought me home. She would give me dinner."

Mrs. Walker's best practices did not go unnoticed and continue today in Joy. As an elementary teacher, Joy shows the same compassion and caring to her first and third grade students, all of whom are English language learners. Most are immigrants who face difficult socio-economic challenges. Joy can relate. She grew up in an impoverished, unstable family. That is why she works tirelessly with, and for, her students. "Being a teacher is much more than teaching students, but an opportunity to inspire, encourage and support others to become the best they can be," explains Joy.

In addition to teaching, Joy serves as a mentor and role model for aspiring teachers through her work with Arizona State University. She also remains very involved in her school, acting as technology integration specialist, mentor teacher, and a curriculum coordinator. In 2010, Joy was recognized as Arizona State Teacher of the Year for her vigorous and impactful work with young people and fellow teachers.

Joy earned her bachelor's degree in early childhood education from Arizona State University and her master's degree in education, curriculum, and instruction from Northern Arizona University. She was also bestowed an honorary doctorate by Northern Arizona University.

**Teacher Top 5**

1. *Believe in Yourself!*: No matter how prepared or seasoned an educator, teaching is challenging. Joy declares, "Teaching is not as easy as many think, [but] it starts with believing that you can make a difference one child at a time, one day at a time." To be a successful teacher, this belief is vitally important. Even though the goal is often to nurture student growth, improve scores, and meet state standards, getting it all done can take time. So, patience is a virtue and a teacher must have a "Never say die" attitude. Joy says, "You have to believe that you're making a difference. It starts with you, and you grow from there." She also points out that teachers can often be isolated in their own classrooms without any other adults to rebound ideas. Don't be

discouraged. Rather, Joy encourages teachers to believe in their own abilities and trust themselves.

2. *Believe in your Students!*: All too often, academic test scores are used to define a student. Joy does not believe that test scores tell the whole picture. In fact, she says, "I don't think it shows what we're capable of. Some of us are just bad test takers." Joy looks at the whole child. Citing Howard Gardner's theory of Multiple Intelligences, Joy believes that students possess other strengths from musical to bodily-kinesthetic. While students may be weak in one area, they may be strong in another. She states, "Students enter our classrooms with many different strengths and weaknesses, and we must take those strengths and enhance them, while using their weaknesses to promote additional growth." The key point is to see students beyond an academic score, find their potential, and hone it. This can only be accomplished if teachers truly believe in their students. "Every child deserves the best education we can provide, and we must believe that they can do it, regardless of any test, any past, anything that says otherwise!" proclaims Joy.

3. *Build Relationships with your Students and their Families*: Joy is fully aware that well-established relationships are the key for success in any situation, but especially in and out of the classroom. Joy notes, "For many students, the teacher is their strongest supporter and greatest ally." Working with English speaking students is difficult enough, but in Joy's case, new immigrants who are English language learners can be even trickier. Language, culture, and the newness of an American education add to the complexities of building relationships.

So how does Joy resolve these issues? She builds rapport by focusing on trust in her classroom, but like her kindergarten teacher, Mrs. Walker, Joy also performs home visits. "My goal is once per week or at least once per month [to do home visits] depending on my schedule," says Joy. Home visits allow parent relationships to develop. It shows how much Joy really cares. "I build relationships through working with the parent where they're at and providing support for whatever I can do in my own limited capacity," says Joy. Oftentimes, parents are not available during school hours. She adds, "I believe that it takes a community and village to raise children and to provide for them emotionally, physically, academically, and socially." While home visits may not be common for most teachers, Joy shares that this is one of the best things that teachers can do to build relationships. In her own background, Joy remembers, "It was my teachers who kept me going as I was growing up. If it wasn't for my teachers, I wouldn't have landed where I did. I try to give back the same way."

4. _Celebrate, Celebrate, Celebrate!_: In many instances, there is an overemphasis on standards, curriculum, and test scores. Joy notices, "We forget that students are human beings and we're not producing cars." Joy is a teacher who works with students from Somalia, Burma, Afghanistan, Iraq, and Mexico. Many of these children do not know the English language and have never been at school. Some do not have any parents. "If you make it to school on time with no parents and you're six years old, that's pretty impressive. I'm going to celebrate and honor that you came that day to be with me to learn," says Joy.

It is imperative to celebrate where these children are and where they are going. Joy remembers a prior student who was 10 years old, never attended school, and did not know English. Joy recalls celebrating every letter of the alphabet that he gained. She states, "That celebration is going to be what motivates him to read." It is the celebration that makes learning fun and gives children the validation that they are doing something positive. In the end, this is what will compel students to continue learning for life. Joy exclaims, "Learning doesn't stop when we leave a classroom, it continues until we die. I want my students to recognize this and embrace the opportunities that come from learning!"

5. *Plan, Prepare, and Provide*: "If I am to help my students become and stay successful, I must plan for their learning, prepare them for their future, and provide multiple opportunities and multiple ways of achieving those goals and achieving those dreams," says Joy. When it comes to teaching, it is important to remember that all students learn differently. Therefore, teachers should not be teaching the same way to everyone. Instead, teaching through multiple modalities is essential. Teachers need to find what learning style works best for each student. Joy comments, "It can't be a one-size-fits-all education… [and] it shouldn't be a just do another worksheet [type of activity]." Teachers must be astute and provide student choice in learning.

**Other Interview Questions**
*1. Who is/are your role model(s) from an educational perspective?*

"My biggest role model was my own kindergarten teacher, Mrs. Walker," says Joy. The constant, unconditional love and genuine support shown by Mrs. Walker was like no other. For instance, when Joy was in sixth grade, her family was destitute. Joy remembers Mrs. Walker coming to her house and bringing food for her family. That's the kind of person she was. Over the course of Joy's life, she maintained close contact with Mrs. Walker. This lasted for 30 years until Mrs. Walker's recent passing.

Joy also identifies her other teachers as role models. Joy comments, "Not only Mrs. Walker, but all my teachers gave me something to take a hold and use as I prepared for my own teaching career." Lastly, Joy mentions her colleagues and administrators. "I learn as much from others as I do from my own students. I have amazing respect for those who are in my profession, and without them, I wouldn't be where I am today," responds Joy.

*2. When you take a look at teachers, in general, and recognize all the hard work and devotion they put into their jobs, what would you say is the one thing that you think teachers can improve upon so they can become more highly effective?*

The changing family structure and dynamic influx of immigrants contribute to the duties of educators beyond the classroom. Joy states, "With today's vast majority of English language learners, high mobility rates, lack of parental involvement, economics, and refugee students coming into schools, things can alter test scores and those don't paint the whole picture. They are a snapshot of what's going on."

Needless to say, test scores are only one measure to determine instructional efficacy. What policy-makers should be looking at is student growth. During an academic year, where did the student begin and where are they now? What are the other things that teachers are doing to contribute to a child's success, including their social, emotional, and physical needs? In order to improve their effectiveness, teachers need to share their voice with decision-makers. Joy states, "I think the one thing teachers can improve upon is being more of a voice in their profession about what they are doing and hold more conversations with politicians, community members, and the public about what is happening. We are often so focused on our students and what it means to them for us that we don't always step outside that box and let our voices be heard loudly about all we are doing."

Joy asserts that a measure of a teacher's success has much more to do than test scores. She continues, "There are very, very few teachers who are not effective or don't put in the hard work that the other 99% do, but we [as a society] are so focused on test scores as the measure of effectiveness. What about the teacher who takes food and clothing to, and pays the electric bill for, her student's family, or the teacher who soothes, bandages, and supports the student with an injury or illness and visits him or her in the hospital, or the teacher who visits the homes of her students weekly just to touch base and build relationships? Are they less effective than the teacher who has high test scores? Absolutely not!"

*3. Are there policies that your school (or past school) has adopted which allow teachers to excel?*

In lieu of an agrarian-based school calendar, Joy's school district moved to an academic calendar with more school days. Joy notes, "We have changed our calendar to 200 school days (the longest in the country), extended our school day, and created weekly opportunities and time to receive professional development so that we can improve our instruction and student achievement simultaneously." This school calendar change has improved student assessment scores and alleviated daycare needs for parents during the historical summer months. Totaling all the additional academic time, students will have attended an extra year's worth of school, counting from kindergarten to eighth grade. In terms of professional development, Joy says, "My district put policies into place through partnerships with the Arizona K-12 center to help teachers receive master teacher status and National Board Certification."

*4. In order to improve our educational system, what are the shortcomings you notice in schools. What are some of the good things happening? What do you think needs to change?*

Joy declares, "When we talk about shortcomings, we fail to recognize the great things happening around us. Negative ideas and focuses don't create solutions. I don't think there is a lot of shortcomings from schools themselves, but our state policies (e.g., assessments) and funding system have created issues that make it very difficult to give our students the best they can."

In Joy's perspective, there are good things happening in education. She shares, "We are moving toward a common understanding of what makes students successful and embracing the idea that less is more, and more is no more! For too long, we have been given the very daunting task of teaching lots of concepts in very short periods so students were getting surface level knowledge…we are moving to the idea that we need to go in depth, not breadth." That way, students gain mastery of concepts. In the past, state standards compelled teachers to teach too quickly in order to touch on all concepts required. This was a disservice to students, because it did not allow enough time for retained comprehension. The instituting of

Common Core State Standards is a positive step, since it explicitly and clearly delineates what students are expected to learn and know at a specific grade.

Lastly, Joy believes that collaboration amongst teachers is slowly becoming ubiquitous. Joy says, "[T]eachers [are] collaborating more and working to support each other. We are no longer thinking in terms of 'my students,' but 'our students' and what can we do as a team to achieve." After all, it takes a village to educate the next generation.

# CHAPTER 3

## Jon Rolle

District of Columbia State Teacher of the Year (2011)
(Elementary – Grades 3 to 5)

*"The ultimate measure of a man is not where he stands in moments of comfort and*
*convenience, but where he stands at times of challenge and controversy."*
— Dr. Martin Luther King, Jr.

Born in Prince George's County, Maryland, Jon Rolle has first-hand experience in overcoming socio-economic obstacles and demographic challenges. He knows that facing them directly is the truest test of any person's mettle. That's why Jon chose Dr. King's powerful words as his favorite quote. Jon attests, "The man that I ultimately am, and want to become, is based on my ideals, morals, and actions during the times in my life that are most challenging, not the ones that are most successful."

So, how does Jon bring his life's philosophy into his classroom? It is through high expectations. He states, "Not every student is going to come in with the tools that they need at the start to be successful. So, the teacher will face a lot of challenges and controversy with the kids that he or she is going teach. With kids, you have to maintain high expectations." That way, each student will meet or exceed his or her goals. With respect to parents and the school, Jon advocates, "Stay true to your foundational beliefs [so you can]...provide the best education needed."

## Background

In Robert Frost's *The Road Not Taken*, he writes, "Two roads diverged in a wood, and I – I took the one less traveled by, And that has made all the difference." Jon Rolle has done that and then some. When Jon graduated from North Carolina State University with a business degree, he intended to go to law school with a focus on intellectual property law. He also thought about becoming a sports agent which would have led to a lucrative career. Becoming a teacher was never in the cards, but Jon's path took him to the education sector. He was encouraged to apply to Teach for America. From the very onset, Jon loved teaching and never looked back.

Most of the time, a career path in education begins as a teacher and, thereafter, leads to administration. Jon's journey, on the other hand, was the reverse. He started out serving in administrative capacities such as Transition Team Coordinator, Learning Team Leader, and Curriculum Specialist. Eventually, Jon became a Program Director for Teach for America and Dean of Students at a public charter school. What was missing in his past positions though, was his desire to put into practice what he learned – research focused on the perception of masculinity and how it affects children in school – from his master's in urban education at the University of Pennsylvania. Jon remembers, "I expressed an interest to my principal…in having an all boy class to see if there was any value to grouping boys together." He adds, "[There is] a deficit of strong, positive, Black male role models." Jon wanted to be that role model to teach the skills necessary for today's youth. Hence, he transitioned into a classroom teacher.

One of Jon's fundamental educational philosophies is "setting high, unwavering expectations…to overcome tough social economic situations." Needless to say, it worked wonders with many of his classes, achieving some of the highest scores in a variety of assessments.

In 2011, Jon was recognized as the District of Columbia's State Teacher of the Year. For a number of years, he has also been a finalist for the Southeast Elementary Academy Teacher of the Year. He also served as keynote speaker for numerous engagements, including the United States Department of Education Health Schools Grant Conference and Teach for America Alumni Induction.

When asked about his decision to follow his heart into teaching versus the financial rewards of the private sector, Jon shares that his reward comes in a very different package, knowing that he has in some way elevated others and contributed to their successes. Jon is a graduate of North Carolina State University with a bachelor's degree in business management. He also holds a master's in education from the University of Pennsylvania.

**Teacher Top 5**

1. _Invest in Parent Interaction_: As a business major in college, Jon sees parents as consumers and education as the product. That explains why Jon wants parents to know as much as possible about their children's education. That way, parents will be willing to invest themselves as parent-teacher partners and engage actively in the school. Parent buy-in is paramount to ensure that what is taught by the teacher in class is reinforced by the parents at home. Jon recommends, "Get parent involvement early. If messages are different (between teacher and parent), it is harder for the teacher to accomplish the goals that are needed to be successful."

To establish this relationship, Jon communicates all policies clearly via a comprehensive, outlined document that is brought home by students and signed by parents. This syllabus-style document stipulates: what will be studied; what are the academic expectations; and what is expected of students (how they act, speak, walk, etc.). At the beginning of the year, Jon also presents an informative "Back to School Night" presentation which provides an overview of the academic year. Throughout the school year, Jon sends home a weekly newsletter which includes academic updates, classroom happenings, and parent volunteer opportunities. Jon often calls home to talk to parents about his students. He points out, "It is important to call about positive things, not only negative."

2. _Apply Academic Rigor_: Since teachers are often filling in gaps of learning from previous years, Jon says, "It is very important to be

aware what is rigorous at the appropriate grade level." There is a tendency to contextualize the student. In other words, a student might be at the top of the class in his or her school, but might be at the near bottom for a school in another county. The context to where students are, and need to be, must be kept in mind. Jon comments, "[Teachers] must have a clear vision and idea for what the student sitting in front of you should be able to know, do, and show."

In order to make sure the appropriate academic rigor is established in the classroom, teachers must have strong content knowledge. Jon states, "Teachers must know their content and what they're teaching." He continues, "One thing good about Common Core [State Standards Initiative] is that it makes sequentially what kids should know before [a specific grade level] and after." As it states directly from the core standards website, Common Core "provide[s] a consistent, clear understanding of what students are expected to learn, so teachers and parents know what they need to do to help them."

3. _Maintain High Expectations_: In order to overcome socio-economic adversity, high expectations need to exist. Jon asserts, "Teachers have to believe, truly, that all students have the right to, and can achieve, a quality education." High expectations promote good decision-making, resulting in high achievements. "The foundation for high expectations," Jon claims, "is being open to showing respect to the kids you are teaching; being open to respecting the parents and community; being willing and humble enough to say that, I do genuinely care about your success."

Every student's educational path will be different. Jon notes, "Some will drive coast to coast in a straight line. Others will take 95 detours.

[That said] even when it's hard to do or say, you must maintain high expectations." That goes for all students whether they have special needs, behavioral problems, or family issues.

4. *Develop Content Knowledge*: While the foundations and fundamentals of some content will be taught similarly through the years, Jon knows that certain ways of learning and teaching have changed dramatically. For that reason, Jon states, "It's important to be a continual learner." As a third grade teacher, Jon recognizes, "There is a big difference between thinking you know third grade math and teaching third grade math." For instance, when Jon teaches multiplication, he knows five to six different ways to teach the concept. One of those techniques might be the strategy that clicks with a particular student. Jon comments, "If I wasn't a continuous learner, I may not know multiple ways to reach different types of learners."

For teachers, Jon knows that it sometimes requires humility to seek instructional guidance in order to improve. However, by doing so, the teacher will become a far more effective educator. In his past experience, Jon identified the Marzano Research Lab and the Teacher's College Readers and Writers Workshop as two highly effective teacher development programs.

5. *Build Student Relationships*: "You can't get through to kids, if they don't feel like you care about them," declares Jon. This applies to any classroom and grade level. He also shares, "It doesn't mean you need to be the kid's friend. My kids knew I was going to be tough on them, but if they needed a hug, they could get one from me." In addition, being authentic is essential. "Kids can see through who is false," claims Jon. "Don't be someone you're not, because it will wear you

down and [eventually] affect the student-teacher relationship." As a third grade teacher, Jon found a balance between his personal voice and teacher voice which are two very different things. For example, Jon uses sarcasm in his personal life, but he feels that is not appropriate for young people. Therefore, he had to reconcile characteristics about himself to match the teacher he wanted to be. He explains, "I see kids as little people. I think about the things they need to feel connected to someone, and try to find the space and opportunities to do that."

**Other Interview Questions**

*1. Who is/are your role model(s) from an educational perspective?*

Jon credits all the people who provided amazing support for him through his journey in education as his role models. This includes, but is not limited to, teachers who taught him in the past who he now attempts to emulate; professors who encouraged self-reflection of his own teaching; and colleagues who are effective in the classroom. Jon states, "As a teacher and administrator, when you can walk into a classroom and see kids and teachers putting the rubber to the road and getting it done...those are the role models."

Jon also identifies Marva Collins, the legendary Chicago educator who founded Westside Preparatory School in an impoverished neighborhood of Chicago, as a role model of great magnitude. He states, "I admire the work of...Marva Collins who worked for students by any means necessary." What makes all of these educators so special, Jon says, is that they have "an innate passion for students and achievement."

*2. When you take a look at teachers, in general, and recognize all the hard work and devotion they put into their jobs, what would you say is the one thing that you think teachers can improve upon so they can become more highly effective?*

As a teacher and a coach of teachers, Jon believes that the one thing to be improved upon is different for every educator. Therefore, it needs to remain fluid. In fact, he conveys that it is different based on where teachers are in their career and location in the country. It is difficult to pinpoint one specific item. Jon, however, does believe that teacher improvement probably falls within his *Teacher Top 5* that he has identified above.

*3. Are there policies that your school (or past school) has adopted which allow teachers to excel?*

There are several policies that have supported teacher development, including the availability and use of technology, reclamation of teacher evaluation systems, and establishment of content mastery circles.

Jon sees technology as a great supplement and way to help students excel. That said, technology should not be conducted teacher-free. He notes that Promethean Boards exist in many classrooms, giving teachers accessibility and flexibility to engage students and interact collaboratively. Smart Labs, which consists of Lego technology and robots, also offers students exposure to engineering and technology.

In the past, teacher evaluation systems were more punitive and less about developing teachers. While this continues to be the case, Jon believes there is a shift in thinking by making it a process about what teachers can improve. At his school, administrators and teachers defined strands of what excellent teaching and learning are. From there, they identified where teachers can improve based on those strands.

Content mastery circles are small, collaborative groups of teachers from different schools who teach the same grade and content. At Jon's district, these circles meet every other week, discussing ways to be more successful, rehearsing lessons, providing accountable feedback, and reviewing assessments to check for rigor.

*4. In order to improve our educational system, what are the shortcomings you notice in schools. What are some of the good things happening? What do you think needs to change?*

In regards to shortcomings, Jon identifies the lack of innovation among antiquated teachers and the need for administrators who can truly lead a school toward success. Jon states, "Teachers who have taught the same concept year after year, must think about how to innovate, make it better each year, and make it fresh." After all, the status quo is not acceptable if student achievement is not high. In terms of administration, Jon believes that the principal needs to be an ambassador in the community, retain a strong command of pedagogy and instruction, and know what it takes to motivate kids academically. Most importantly, Jon says, "The ability to inspire is the biggest piece." He continues, "People don't quit the job, they quit their boss…if they don't like their boss, Johnny is standing on a chair, and a parent just gave them an earful, then why should they stay?" The right administrative person is mission critical for any school to succeed.

As for positives, Jon points out that the rise of charter schools have been important, giving parents and kids the opportunity for choice. Teach for America is a good model of successful charters. That said, Jon states, "Charter and public schools need to work collaboratively to make sure all kids are getting the education they deserve. Just opening up charter schools and having them be successful, while public schools suffer, isn't going to do anyone justice in the long run." He also identifies strong teacher networks as a positive way to collaborate. Jon touts the National Network of State Teacher of the Year as very meaningful.

# CHAPTER 4

## Lee-Ann Stephens
Minnesota State Teacher of the Year (2007)
(English Language Arts – Grades 5 to 6)

*"Nobody got anywhere in the world by simply being content."*

— *Louis L'Amour*

Lee-Ann Stephens is the epitome of a lifelong learner who is always striving to better herself as an educator. She loves Louis L'Amour's quote, because it shows that positive, forward movement does not happen unless the individual puts himself or herself into a situation that allows for growth. For Lee-Ann, this often means delving into an uncomfortable area in order to stretch. She states, "When you're content, you're not making any changes. Nothing happens, if you are content where you are."

So what is Lee-Ann's suggestion? Lee-Ann offers, "My philosophy is that it's more important for me to be uncomfortable, so that my students are comfortable." For this reason, Lee-Ann is always seeking ways to meet her students "where they are." It is not simply delivering instruction. Rather, it is about building relationships with students. In fact, it can also mean riding the bus home with kids who need that extra mentoring. "Teaching is about giving [students] the skills to make it through the day, week, or rest of their lives," Lee-Ann confides, "And if I'm content, that means I'm a little too comfortable and I'm not moving forward." She adds, "Teaching is knowing that to the world, I may be one teacher; but to one student, I may be the world."

**Background**

Lee-Ann Stephens is the model success story of a career changer. When Lee-Ann first graduated from college, she worked as an associate buyer for Dayton-Hudson, a then-leading department store in the United States. However, teaching offered Lee-Ann the chance to meet a higher calling. In becoming a teacher, she comments, "We really do affect lives…who's going to remember me for picking out the right dress for someone?" She adds, "I feel that teaching called me, and I answered the call."

As a classroom teacher, Lee-Ann's passion was visibly apparent. She attributes her love for teaching in part to Joelle McIlroy, her high school teacher. Lee-Ann recounts, "Joelle established a relationship with me. She took it beyond the classroom and her interest in me had a profound impact on my life." Like Joelle, Lee-Ann did the same for her students. Lee-Ann knew each and everyone like they were her own children. In many respects, her classroom felt like one big family.

In her 25 years of experience in schools, Lee-Ann has worn many hats, including classroom teacher in urban and suburban school districts, one of the founding teachers of the KIPP Stand Academy, and administrative roles such as Director of Students and High Achievement Program Advocate. For her exemplary work, Lee-Ann was named the 2007 Minnesota's State Teacher of the Year. In 2010, Tim Pawlenty, the former Minnesota Governor, appointed Lee-Ann to the Minnesota Board of Teaching. To date, she continues to serve in a number of leadership positions.

Lee-Ann holds a bachelor's degree in elementary education and a master's degree in curriculum and instruction from the University of Minnesota. She also earned a bachelor's degree in international studies from Miami University. Currently, Lee-Ann is pursuing her doctorate in educational leadership.

**Teacher Top 5**

1. _Do Whatever It Takes_: All students learn differently and many of them have schedules that do not coincide with that of their teacher. For this reason, Lee-Ann believes in "do[ing] whatever it takes to ensure the success of [her] students." At the very beginning of the school year, Lee-Ann gives her personal cell phone number to the class. That way, students can reach her as needed. Lee-Ann remembers a student whose mother could not help with homework, because she had intellectual disabilities. Lee-Ann allowed this student to call her every night for help with homework. She asserts, "My response

as a teacher is to do whatever I can to help her succeed. If it meant talking to her every evening, I'm going to do that." In addition, Lee-Ann often gives up weekends to assist her students. Many of her high school students cannot meet with Lee-Ann during regular school hours due to schedule conflicts. As a result, Lee-Ann hosts study groups on Sundays in order to ensure student success. She comments, "If it means nights or weekends, I do it. I adjust my schedule to meet their needs."

2. _Eliminate the Blame Game_: Blaming outside factors such as a student's home life, parent situation, and socio-economic status lowers expectations. Low student expectations often condone justification for poor performance. Lee-Ann states, "If I rely on blaming outside factors, then I absolve myself from my responsibility as a teacher." That is not what teaching is. She adds, "Poor people can achieve." Lee-Ann hones in on the things which she can control. She asks, "Am I giving my absolute best?" To reach a variety of learners, perhaps looking at a lesson plan differently might help. Maybe the delivery needs to be adjusted. No matter what, teachers need to make sure that they are doing everything that they can possibly do.

When Lee-Ann was given a sixth grade remedial math and language arts class – with 27 students and only six at grade level – to teach, she did not lament. Instead, her attitude was, "The only way to go is up." Unlike some other classes where students were more independent, Lee-Ann was very heavily involved, always interfacing and engaging students. While it was challenging, she claims, "It was one of my best years." At the end of the year, 23 of her 27 students were at grade level or above. Better yet, there was no blame game.

3. _Struggling Students Deserve the Highest Quality of Teaching_: Struggling students are often the most challenging and are known to frustrate the teacher. Therefore, many teachers send these students to read or work with a paraprofessional or parent volunteer. Lee-Ann frowns upon this practice. She declares, "If you struggle, you need me. You need the best instructor...the students that excel can work with the paraprofessional and parents." After all, it is the teacher's responsibility to address challenges head-on as opposed to pawning it off to someone else.

Moreover, Lee-Ann retains a unique philosophy when working with different ability groups. In reading, for example, above-grade level students field open-ended questions to develop critical thinking skills. For below-grade level students, Lee-Ann does the same. Even though she recognizes that these students are very literal and concrete in their comprehension, Lee-Ann believes that they need to develop their critical thinking skills too. Watering down questions for easy to find answers is not the solution. Lee-Ann emphasizes, "It's not everyone's philosophy, but I feel very strongly about it."

4. _If My Students Fail, Then I Have Failed_: High teacher standards are imperative for student learning. In class, it is inevitable that a few students will struggle with a certain concept. At the same time though, Lee-Ann states, "If half of my class fails a test, then I've failed in my job as a teacher." She points out, "If they didn't learn it, then you probably did a presentation. You presented information. You didn't teach it." Lee-Ann insists on making certain students understand the information and providing multiple opportunities to do better. She adds, "It's not about too bad for you, or I gotcha." Teaching is about helping students learn from their mistakes.

41

In her classroom, Lee-Ann has a "Parking Lot" in-box whereby students can anonymously submit queries about lessons or concepts. She takes these submissions and then reteaches, as need be, the next morning. Lee-Ann also utilizes "Exit Slips" to check for understanding. At the end of math class, for instance, she asks students to summarize what they learned. This way, Lee-Ann can prepare students to be successful.

5. _Respect and Love Your Students Like Your Own Children_: "Relationships are key," says Lee-Ann, "I can't teach effectively without knowing my students." Unlike many teachers who perform surveys and such, Lee-Ann's strategy is to spend time and truly get to know them. Aside from class, she joins students at lunch and recess. She also attends athletic games and music recitals. Even though she has a family of her own, Lee-Ann makes time, because strong connections are imperative and she makes it her business to know her students.

For students of color, in particular, Lee-Ann points out, "One thing they can do is not learn from you, even if it impacts them in a negative way. They can totally shut down. That's why relationships are so important. They need to know that I'm authentic and I really care for them." If that student-teacher bond is formed, then students will do what you say because they know the teacher means well. She adds, "When I say, 'Boy, you need to sit down and get busy,' they don't take offense." Instead, the student response is often, "Mrs. Stephens loves me." Interestingly enough, Lee-Ann had lunch with a former student she first taught 22 years ago. The two most important things he said was, "You taught me how to read, and you are like my second mom."

## Other Interview Questions

*1. Who is/are your role model(s) from an educational perspective?*

Lee-Ann's grandmother, Aurelia Ruffin, is her role model. She was not simply an educator. She was a shining example of the commitment and desire to teach. Lee-Ann recounts, "When [Aurelia] was first hired back in 1949, she was in need of one class. Therefore, the school district didn't pay her until she was able to take the course." Unfortunately without a paycheck, Aurelia could not afford the needed class. Lee-Ann notes, "She still taught everyday and did a phenomenal job. She taught for five months without receiving a paycheck. My grandmother went to work every day, as if she were getting paid. She is my inspiration." In the end, Lee-Ann's great grandparents gave Aurelia the money to pay for the course. Lee-Ann states, "[Aurelia's] tenacity reminds us just how important this work is."

*2. When you take a look at teachers, in general, and recognize all the hard work and devotion they put into their jobs, what would you say is the one thing that you think teachers can improve upon so they can become more highly effective?*

While every teacher is not innately a relationship person, Lee-Ann stresses the importance of developing this skill. She states, "If the teacher has built a relationship with the student, then teaching becomes so much easier." Lee-Ann believes that building rapport can be as simple as noticing a new haircut or pair of shoes, giving a smile, or welcoming students at the door upon arrival. Making sure body language and facial expressions match is also important. If there is a disconnect, students pick up on it immediately. Lee-Ann also encourages showing respect in order to get respect. She also tells students openly that it is a privilege and honor to teach them.

Lee-Ann believes that it is essential to see who the students can become, and not necessarily who they are at that moment. She remembers a past student who entered her class with severe behavioral and learning difficulties. Due to the daily student challenges, Lee-Ann drove to the boy's house to meet with his mother. On the way there, Lee-Ann thought deeply about what she wanted to say, considering the student's problems in class. When they met, the mother stood behind a screen door with her son standing behind her. Both mother and son were apprehensive. Then, Lee-Ann shared, "I just came to let you know how glad I am to have your son in class. I'm looking forward to the year with him." Even though she was not speaking the exact truth, Lee-Ann saw the student she wanted him to be and not the student he was. Furthermore, Lee-Ann projected onto the mother what Lee-Ann wanted to see in him, speaking in the present tense, and not future. The next day at school, Lee-Ann comments, "The student was a different child and we had a great year." Building this type of relationship was a game changer. Lee-Ann exclaims, "Ten to fifteen years from now, they will remember very little of what I taught them, but they will remember how I made them feel."

*3. Are there policies that your school (or past school) has adopted which allow teachers to excel?*

Lee-Ann cites that much of the motivation that compels her to excel and be the best she can be is derived from within. She points out that there is a lack of incentive for teachers to be great. This is exacerbated by the chemical DNA of many educators. Lee-Ann describes, "Nobody [teachers] wants to stand out. That's the problem. We have to have people who want to stand out. Otherwise, how do you have models of what good teaching looks like?" Teaching is also a profession that should be compensated fairly. She claims, "A lot of other professions are more valued financially in society." Needless to say, that needs to change.

If she could establish policy her way, Lee-Ann would love to have a master teacher in every classroom alongside a developing teacher. She states, "A master teacher is someone who has shown himself or herself to be effective and innovative. It doesn't matter how many years they've taught….Having taught a lot of years doesn't make you exceptional." Master teachers would be instrumental in providing high quality instruction and guiding others.

*4. In order to improve our educational system, what are the shortcomings you notice in schools. What are some of the good things happening? What do you think needs to change?*

The major shortcoming Lee-Ann notices is the blaming of outside factors pertaining to the lack of achievement by students. By doing so, it absolves the teacher of responsibility. Any and all pre-conceived notions, biases, and assumptions must be eliminated so that students have the opportunity to reach their full potential.

As for the good things, Lee-Ann identifies, "We have teachers looking at equity in their classrooms and examining how their biases may have contributed to the racial achievement gap. We are seeing more and more students of color in advanced courses. We are integrating technology more and more in the classrooms. We are recognizing that this isn't a one-size-fits-all system; therefore, we are offering more choices for students and their families."

# CHAPTER 5

**Jason Fulmer**
National Teacher of the Year Finalist (2004)
(Elementary – Grade 3)

*"Success in life has nothing to do with what you gain in life or accomplish*
*for yourself. It's what you do for others."*

— Danny Thomas

Jason Fulmer's upbringing has always allowed him to see and practice the big picture: altruism. It began with his parents and followed with his teachers. Jason says, "Throughout my life experiences, from church to extracurricular activities, I have had mentors who have demonstrated the importance of giving. In college, I had the opportunity to serve in a variety of leadership roles with organizations like

Circle K, the collegiate version of Kiwanis. The University of South Carolina Aiken really focused on community partners and performed worthwhile deeds. These experiences really changed me and formed my philosophy. I truly found great reward in giving back to my community."

Jason's belief is that people must look beyond themselves, consider the needs of the world, and think about ways they can serve. He comments, "I have often said when I was selected as Teacher of the Year that it's not about the title. It's about the opportunity to serve and give back to a system that has given so much to me." That is why Jason thinks it is so important to collaborate with colleagues, be active in the community, and work with local leaders. Most importantly, students must be inspired, because they are the future of tomorrow. Jason adds, "We have to help kids see service before self. I think that's the only way we can move forward as a nation." In terms of teaching, Jason states, "I'm really proud to be a teacher and cannot think of a better profession to give back through service as an educator."

**Background**

When Indiana Jones in *Raiders of the Lost Ark* said, "It's not the years, it's the miles," he could have been speaking about Jason Fulmer. In just four brief years of teaching experience, Jason was named South Carolina's Teacher of the Year. Perhaps Jason was selected for "Giving feet to dreams" to his students, since he considers teaching a dream-developing business. Then again, it might have been his innovative teaching style. As a singing teacher, he rewrote lyrics of familiar songs in order to teach students who were struggling with math, spelling, and other subjects. Either way, Jason's wisdom about how to reach students best is that of an old soul. He understands that good teaching makes all the difference in the world and that teaching is not a job that provides instant gratification. Jason states, "It may be years later before you realize the impact you've had on a child, but knowing you have made a difference in the life of one student matters."

Since winning his state's Teacher of the Year award and being named as one of the four finalists for National Teacher of the Year, Jason segued from in-class student instruction to teacher mentoring initiatives and leading various professional development programs. He understands the challenges new and seasoned teachers face as well as the rewards that come from changing students' lives through effective teaching. Currently, Jason serves as Program Director for Mentoring and Teacher Leadership at the Center for Educator Recruitment, Retention and Advancement in South Carolina. Even with his new responsibilities, Jason always remembers his third graders from Redcliffe Elementary School in Aiken, South Carolina. In fact, he has made it a priority to attend each graduating ceremony for previous classes he taught and special life events along the way. Jason shares, "I always told my students that once they're my kids, they're always my kids."

Among his many accolades, Jason points out that the Redcliffe Teacher of the Year Award was one of the most humbling. He states, "To be selected by your peers is one of the greatest honors. Everything else has been icing on the cake." Jason received a bachelor's degree in elementary education from the University of South Carolina Aiken. He also holds a master's degree in educational leadership from Augusta State University.

## Teacher Top 5

1. *You Must Reach Them, Before You Can Teach Them!*: All excellent teachers know how important it is to establish solid student-teacher and parent-teacher relationships. Jason declares, "In this age of instant connectivity, it's easy to lose the power of the personal touch." The value of human connections is still very important, even though technology has enhanced and facilitated communication. That's why Jason takes the extra time to make phone calls and write personal handwritten notes. "Communication is a lost art and people want to know they matter; you care about them and their students," says Jason. Prior to the start of school, Jason details, "I would…send post cards to the families over the summer that describe a little bit about what third grade would be like. At pre-open house, I'd have a science fair board with a picture of me on it from when I was in third grade so the kids can see that I was just like them, and a part of the same learning process."

The result from this ongoing relationship building is a foundation of trust to begin learning. Jason says, "Take the time to establish relationships and trust early on…when your kids come in those first few days, it becomes all about building upon those relationships as opposed to creating new ones." Teachers must understand each student's background, what he or she loves to do, and what makes each student tick. By doing so, connections can be cemented to make success come to life for every pupil. Jason comments, "That often used saying, 'You have to reach them before you can teach them,' is very much the case."

2. *Set the Stage for Learning*: Too often, students walk into a classroom with commercial-made posters and generic academic placards

with nothing to engage and inspire students. Jason believes in creating a personalized environment so that students are excited to come to school. He states, "I want them to walk into a comfortable, inviting classroom that welcomes discovery and stimulates learning.... Highly inviting and cozy classrooms invite people to learn and keep them coming back every day for more."

In his first year of teaching, Jason was assigned an old, distant portable trailer that had not been painted since the 1980s. To set the stage for learning, Jason created something close to his heart, a beach themed classroom painted with fresh cool colors, hanging fishnets in the windows, beach chairs on the floor, and a reading island. At a pre-open house, one student exclaimed, "This place looks like Red Lobster, I'm going to love it!" Jason says, "The small things make a difference....I wanted my kids to dream as large as the ocean."

3. _Differentiate Instruction_: "Differentiated instruction is really thinking about how you can maximize the learning, over what traditionally happens in a one-size-fits-all approach....In my classroom, I utilize the Multiple Intelligences and try to teach the information in a variety of ways. Whether your kids are visual learners, auditory learners, or kinesthetic learners, you have to work to provide that instruction in ways that meet all of their needs," says Jason. A prime example is how Jason assessed for literacy. Since differentiation is about choice, he gives students multiple opportunities to showcase their mastery. In their reading response journals, students can demonstrate comprehension in a variety of ways. Kids can write about a character in the story and use details to support their answer; pretend to be a teacher and create three questions to determine if students read the chapter; illustrate and write a caption for the sections read; and

so forth. The key is to provide lots of different choices. Jason adds, "I utilize grouping to make differentiated instruction more efficient in my classroom…groups must be carefully selected and the learning must be customized….Often some of the richest learning occurs peer-to-peer no matter the age. We must cater our teaching to meet all learning styles and the rich diversity of our students."

4. _Integrate the Arts_: The arts, especially performing and visual, have a way of opening up numerous opportunities for students to succeed. It is supported by brain research and Jason believes, "[It] makes connections for kids and awakens the creative mind which is what we need in the 21st century." One way Jason integrates the arts is by teaching through song and movement. When his third graders were struggling with the use of a number line to round to the nearest ten, Jason rewrote the lyrics of the _Jeffersons_ television theme song. Students sang the newly revised song while moving up and down a number line Jason taped onto the floor. The catchy little tune and the body mapping element helped kids remember the rules for rounding. Later, Jason revised the Supremes' "Stop in the Name of Love" to "Stop I'm an Octagon." His class became a singing lab that created little songs to assist recall of concepts. Jason states, "Music has a way of connecting all of us and I definitely utilize it as a teaching tool in my classroom….What you learn with your body you never forget, because you take it with you everywhere you go. It's easy to fuse movement, music, and your body as well as music, art, and drama… to open up learning possibilities and make it fun for you and your students."

5. _Celebrate Successes_: No matter how large or small, team and individual successes should be celebrated. Jason says, "Tiny victories are

often overlooked, but not in my eyes. Seeing the joy on students' faces when they learn something new, and watching them grow and make wise choices is very rewarding! My classroom newsletter was entitled, 'Footprints.' It stays with the theme of the beach, but signifies learning. Some days we make giant leaps, while other days we make small footsteps toward our goal. My goal is to create footprints in their mind that will inspire them to dream and believe that they can achieve."

Celebrations can take the form of simple, but specific words of encouragement. Other times, it might be performing a cheer such as "Doing the Elvis!" Kids wiggle their hips, pretend to strum a guitar, and say, "Thank you, thank you very much!" It can also be a special speaker in class or even a well-deserved pizza party. All in all, it is not always about getting a prize. Jason sees it as "creating a climate of success where kids are celebrated." Jason shares, "I must help my students take their first step, but then inspire them to continue on their journeys as they find their own pathways to success."

**Other Interview Questions**
*1. Who is/are your role model(s) from an educational perspective?*

The common element around all of Jason's role models is that they left an indelible mark and legacy in the people they touched. Jason's mom and dad were not only his parents, but also his very first teachers. They encouraged, assisted, and always sought to help Jason reach his full ability. Jason says, "Thinking positively and enthusiastically about people and their potential comes natural for me, because my parents, my first teachers in my life, believed in me."

Other role models include the dozens of teachers along Jason's journey through school. "My teachers created a love of learning and the value of community. I can name every single one of my teachers from my K to 12 experiences. Each of them taught me more than mere facts, but how to live. My third grade teacher, Mrs. Watson, believed in me and pushed me to never settle for second best. My seventh grade teacher, Ms. Toepke, made mathematics relevant to my life; she helped me overcome my fear of math and gave me that extra push and encouragement. She is still in touch with me today. My high school English teacher, Mrs. Armstrong, provided me wisdom, modeling every day what it takes to become a quality educator and putting my dream-making into practice....My professors at USC Aiken encouraged me every step of my undergraduate experience to fulfill a childhood dream. They sharpened my skills, while allowing my love and enthusiasm for teaching to blossom," says Jason. Lastly, Jason identifies Deidre Martin, his Circle K advisor, for inspiring him about the importance of giving back to the community.

*2. When you take a look at teachers, in general, and recognize all the hard work and devotion they put into their jobs, what would you say is the one thing that you think teachers can improve upon so they can become more highly effective?*

"Far too often in our career due to challenges, morale and pride in our profession are weak," responds Jason. That is because the teacher's voice is often the missing voice at the decision-making table. It is important to value the voices of all stakeholders in the educational process. Jason comments, "Teachers mold and shape the future; this is not an idealistic statement; it is absolute truth. We are professionals....Pride in our profession is essential." To begin the process, the level of collaboration and shared leadership must be broadened and elevated. Opportunities need to exist that allow teachers to lead not only in the classroom, but beyond the walls too.

On the educator side, Jason points out that teachers must commit and be willing to learn and develop, each and every year. He states, "We don't want teachers to do their first year 30 different times. Each year, we must grow and stretch."

*3. Are there policies that your school (or past school) has adopted which allow teachers to excel?*

During his third year of teaching, Jason initiated a professional learning community in his school called STARS – Supporting Teachers to Achieve, Reach, and Succeed. He states, "After that first year of teaching, I was motivated by my own challenges in the classroom...I had a great mentor, but looking back on induction program experiences, I was isolated in an auditorium where over 100 new teachers attended professional development sessions. What I really needed was a chance to connect with other people and discuss different problems and solutions that related to teaching, versus a one-size-fits-all model of support. What was missing was that peer-to-peer camaraderie where all of us, in similar situations, could discuss ideas and problem solve." STARS was structured so that teachers had the opportunity to collaborate and share practical ideas about specific concepts for success. Jason details, "STARS was not meant to be a gripe session, but an opportunity to share best practices. One month, a discussion might be about classroom management. So your ticket in the door was a technique or strategy that you could share with the group on ways to improve classroom management. Other topics included things like differentiated instruction and various ideas on involving parents."

Going forward, Jason has utilized the STARS model with the mentoring and teacher leadership program at Center for Educator Recruitment, Retention and Advancement in South Carolina. He states, "We are working hard on our mentoring initiative, because it's so important that schools move beyond the buddy system of support. School systems across the country must begin embracing research-based, structured support systems that provide mentors with the tools, strategies, and resources they need to provide tailored quality support....Our goal is not to simply keep new teachers, but to assist in building accomplished teachers who know how to help students succeed....The idea is to get them more involved in the processes that shape their teaching and not just the teaching itself. Any teacher can start a program like STARS and probably should if there isn't already one in place at their school."

*4. In order to improve our educational system, what are the shortcomings you notice in schools. What are some of the good things happening? What do you think needs to change?*

In America, Jason believes that public schools and its access are some of the greatest freedoms in our country. At the same time, he states, "For many years we've looked at public schools in the wrong light. Too many people are focusing on the costs of public schools when they should be shifting their focus and thinking about them as investments: investments in our children, investments in our society, and investments in our nation's democracy....We must promote more accurate dialogue in the public and in the media so that more rational information can be shared. For instance, a report might say that a school is near the bottom in math scores, but if you dig deeper, you might find that that school also has far higher standards for those scores." Jason urges for greater analysis in the way data is reported and examined. He states, "It's important because once you start looking rationally at all of the data, you start to see that public schools are actually performing well in many areas."

When it comes to shortcomings, there are plenty, including accountability, inadequate funding, apathy, dropout rates, the need for uniform standards, and the threat of school violence. Jason responds, "[T]he resolutions are not found in a quick-fix package or program....We can build a bridge by allowing these challenges to make conceivably dramatic improvements in the way we recruit and prepare teachers, support them, and provide for their ongoing learning. What will not change, however, is the need for excellent teachers for every child in America! I'm really passionate about the need to provide quality mentoring and support for all teachers. I think it's critically important to improvement in our schools. The development of teacher leadership initiatives, multiple paths for teachers to serve, and accelerating new teacher development are important for our kids. When we focus on the quality of educators, our students benefit."

As for things that need to change, Jason exclaims, "We must prepare our students to be creative thinkers and problem solvers. Our educational focus must shift from preparing students to perform well on a test, to equipping our students with the skills and knowledge necessary to be successful in an ever-changing world. We are teaching students today who will be leaders in a world that does not yet exist.

With all of the advancements, our students need to be more prepared than ever before to be relational leaders and critical thinkers."

# CHAPTER 6

## Kathleen Brody

Literacy Education Instructor (former) at Teachers College
(Elementary and Special Education – Grades Pre-K to 6)

*"I've come to the frightening conclusion that I am the decisive element in the*
*classroom. It's my daily mood that makes the weather. As a teacher, I possess a*
*tremendous power to make a child's life miserable or joyous. I can be a tool of*
*torture or an instrument of inspiration. I can humiliate or humor, hurt or heal.*
*In all situations, it is my response that decides whether a crisis will be escalated or*
*de-escalated and a child humanized or de-humanized."*

— Dr. Haim Ginott

As an educator who not only teaches children, but also educates
teachers how to teach, Kathy Brody selected Dr. Ginott's quote

because she says, "It speaks to the power that teachers have in the classroom." The teacher is the chief steward whose decisions affect the overall climate of the classroom and learning environment in which students are to prosper.

For many educators, Dr. Ginott is best remembered for his work on how adults should relate to children. While he worked as a renowned clinical psychologist, child therapist, parent educator, and author, Dr. Ginott started out as an elementary school teacher in the late 1940s. In 1965, Dr. Ginott published his best-seller, *Between Parent and Child*, which is still popular today. Dr. Ginott's philosophy of combining compassion and boundary setting is the hallmark of Kathy's own teaching. It gives respect to children's feelings while setting limits on behavior.

**Background**

For over 35 years, Kathy has been involved in just about every aspect of education. Kathy has not only taught students in the classroom in a variety of elementary grade levels, but she has also served as faculty, mentor, and literacy expert to graduate students of education and practicing teachers. In fact, Kathy even successfully started, owned, and directed her own independent school, "the children's place," for 16 years in New York.

With an expertise in literacy, Kathy served as an Instructor at Teachers College in their Literacy Specialist Program. She also was a Staff Developer at Teachers College Reading and Writing Project. In the past, Kathy was also an instructor at the Connecticut Writing Project.

Over the course of her career, Kathy has been involved in a variety of other capacities in education. She worked as a literacy coach at K to 8 schools, a Building Educator Support Teams Mentor for beginning teachers and student teachers, and a presenter at numerous nationwide workshops and conferences.

Perhaps most interestingly, Kathy and her fourth grade class at Six to Six Magnet School in Bridgeport, Connecticut won Scholastic's "Kids Are Authors" contest in 2003. Kathy directed and guided student collaboration in writing and illustrating *Animalogies: A Collection of Animal Analogies*. Since the contest, the picture book has been published by Scholastic. Kathy is also the author of an article, "Growing Writers Through Collaboration," published in the National Writing Project's newsletter, *The Voice*.

Today, Kathy has returned back to her first love, the classroom, where she continues to educate young people and mentor other educators. As Kathy states, "I'm still learning," which keeps teaching fresh, fun, and wonderful.

Kathy holds a bachelor's degree in elementary education from State University of New York, College at Oswego. She also received her master's in special education from State University of New York, College at New Paltz.

## Teacher Top 5

1. _Take Time to Build Community_: In schools, Kathy states, "The social curriculum is just as important as the academic curriculum." The Golden Rule, treating others as you would like to be treated, can only exist if teachers create an environment that is nurturing, open to different ideas, and safe for everyone. In order to understand how to build community, Kathy says, "The Responsive Classroom approach is a good place to start." It stresses student empowerment. Teachers should provide students with as much choice as possible and include them in the classroom process. For instance, the students and teacher should come up with the classroom rules together, creating unity and buy-off as well as facilitating the inner-workings of the classroom.

Establishing rituals is essential to building community. "It not only develops routines and schedules, but it also offers security," describes Kathy. Recognizing what is done at the start of every day, celebrating after a core literature book is completed, and throwing a publishing party following the achievement of an important writing project are all rituals that create a classroom family.

2. _Celebrate the Positive in Each Student_: The power of positive reinforcement is undeniably effective in the classroom. Kathy asserts, "Teachers must recognize students when they are doing well." The age-old saying, "Catch kids being good," promotes appropriate behavior. This especially applies when the teacher models the behavior they want to see in class.

One strategy Kathy utilizes is a "Closing Circle" performed at the end of every day. The entire class gets together as a community, and the teacher starts off by paying a compliment to a specific student. For instance, the teacher states, "Nick, I noticed you remembering to raise your hand today when you wanted to participate in our discussion." Thereafter, students follow and take the lead. Kathy believes that this type of acknowledgment nurtures good behavior which is an important life skill. That said, positive reinforcement should not be relegated to the end of the day. Instead, educators must find and acknowledge each student's strengths throughout the entire day. By doing so, teachers can inform and encourage students to pursue what they are good at. Sometimes, children are unaware of their special talents. Kathy knows that teachers have the unique opportunity to teach students that there is something special about each one of them.

3. _Insert "Fun" into the Day_: "Once routines and rituals are established, teachers should find ways to insert fun into the day," says Kathy. In school, students sit in chairs, but at home they are deluged with an exorbitant amount of tools and activities (e.g., Internet, smart phones, sports) that vie for their attention. Teachers must make learning fun. This can be accomplished through simple humor, personality, and well-developed lessons.

For spelling, as an example, instead of performing the usual paper and pencil monotony, Kathy recounts using shaving cream on kids' tables for spelling words. If managed and taught appropriately for specific age levels, the discipline of spelling can be a weekly highlight for everyone.

4. _Be Self-Reflective in your Work and a Lifelong Learner_: Humility is inextricably tied to self-reflection and lifelong learning. At the end

of every academic day, teachers should ask themselves: What went well? What needs to change? Kathy states, "By self-reflecting and analyzing your craft, teachers can become more successful in their own teaching. It is hard to be a learner, if you think you can do it all." Like the students taught, teachers are always learning too. In addition, good teachers are passionate. Kathy remarks, "Passion is contagious. Weave your passion into your lessons." This coincides with making the learning experience more interesting and personal. For instance, if a teacher loves to rollerblade, then share it with the class. Include it in math lessons and other subjects. There are numerous ways to do this constructively, and the kids will love it!

5. _Collaborate with Others_: In order to be truly successful in the classroom, teachers need to collaborate and talk with other educators. Kathy declares, "The idiom, 'Two heads are better than one,' has plenty of truth." She recommends, "Surround yourself with exemplary people, and find two to three high quality teachers who are willing to share and tap them as resources." Bouncing ideas off of another educator whom a teacher respects allow for greater clarity and understanding. Be selective, but open. Lastly, it is also just as important to give as well as to receive.

**Other Interview Questions**

_1. Who is/are your role model(s) from an educational perspective?_

Ruth Sidney Charney, Fred Rodgers, and Lucy Calkins are Kathy's primary educational role models.

As one of the co-founders of the Responsive Classroom movement, Ruth Sidney Charney has been a powerful inspiration to Kathy. For about a year, Charney worked in Kathy's classroom, sharing her insight and knowledge. For Kathy, this was an incredible opportunity to learn about the Responsive Classroom approach. Kathy states, "The basic premise is not to make assumptions about children in terms of what they know and can do." Rather, the approach consists of practical strategies for helping children build academic and social-emotional competencies day in and day out. At the beginning of the year, teacher expectations are modeled. Thereafter, the nitty-gritty details of teaching are executed in a pragmatic, collaborative, and positive manner. Ruth Sidney Charney, in Kathy's opinion, is one of the best educators who knows how to reach children.

Fred Rodgers, more commonly known as Mr. Rodgers, is another role model. Kathy asserts, "Reading his books, Fred Rodgers communicates the importance of treating children with dignity and respect." Kathy believes that honoring the entire or "whole" child is essential for the teacher, and Fred Rodgers did an amazing job of this.

According to Kathy, Lucy Calkins' work in literacy has been nothing short of brilliant. What she has given teachers to help students read and write has paved the way for a generation of educators. Kathy declares, "I admire the work she [Calkins] has done."

*2. When you take a look at teachers, in general, and recognize all the hard work and devotion they put into their jobs, what would you say is the one thing that you think teachers can improve upon so they can become more highly effective?*

Kathy knows that time management represents one of the most challenging aspects of teaching. In an academic day, time is lost transitioning, securing student attention, and even lining up. Kathy shares, "If you add up all the minutes, a lot of time is simply lost." To remedy this, Kathy believes that teachers must hold students to high standards of time management. This way, instructional time will increase. Kathy suggests that schools identify a specific teacher who is very effective in this capacity. Then, this teacher can serve as a strong model for others to observe.

*3. Are there policies that your school (or past school) has adopted which allow teachers to excel?*

To address the issue of time needed for teacher collaboration, Kathy talks about how one of her schools implemented a formal policy of making time for educators. On the weekly calendar, meetings were scheduled for respective educators such as the homeroom and the English language learner teacher. Depending on their specific schedules, Kathy states, "A learning support person was assigned to cover each person's classroom." This way, time was made for all parties involved, and the collaboration model was fully honored.

Another notable policy involves the collection of teacher plan books by administration. In lieu of doing this, Kathy says, "Administration required a written self-reflection once per month." The reflection topic was chosen by the teacher and was not mandated by administration. Best yet, the principal would provide meaningful and actionable responses to the reflection. In other words, the principal would actually take time to read it, and give constructive analysis and support.

*4. In order to improve our educational system, what are the shortcomings you notice in schools. What are some of the good things happening? What do you think needs to change?*

Shortcomings come in the form of leadership from the principal and the teachers themselves.

In terms of administration, Kathy states, "Principals need to get out of the office and into the classroom." While the demands on, and responsibilities of, principals are vast and wide, almost all of the important action exists in the classroom. Teacher observations are a first step, but constructive feedback is even more important to develop teachers. Kathy also believes that principals need to recognize teachers who are doing a great job. "Teachers want to know that they are valued and appreciated for what they are doing," says Kathy. Recognition does not have to be monetary or a bulletin board showcasing the teacher of the month. Instead, creative forms of gratitude such as a small, hand-written note by the principal left in the mailbox of a teacher, identifying something positive, is appreciation enough. This is similar to the same concept of catching kids being good. Kathy responds, "All of this translates to modeling where teachers can adopt these same strategies, and do the same for their students."

As for teachers, Kathy believes that a greater emphasis on community building needs to exist. Often times, teacher preparation programs singularly focus on theory and academics. At the end of the day, in order for a teacher to be successful, the classroom must run not only smoothly and efficiently, but also encourage risk-taking and participation from everyone. This can only be done by creating a nurturing and safe environment where everyone is accepted and embraced.

Kathy points out that some of the good things happening in schools include mentor programs and professional development. For new teachers, teaching in a classroom can be daunting. Educating students, managing parents, working with administration and peers are all part of a teacher's job description. Individually assigning mentors can make a tremendous difference. Mentors can provide advice and give counsel. Most importantly, mentors can lend a sympathetic ear and relieve the isolation new teachers might feel.

Kathy adds that professional development should be on the top of every educator's list to hone skills and keep current. Many times, professional development is selectively offered. Kathy declares, "This needs to change and be available to all faculty members. At a minimum, every educator should attend a professional development opportunity once per year."

# CHAPTER 7

## Angela Wilson
National Teacher of the Year Finalist (2012)
(Language Arts, Forensics – Grade 7)

*"It is an honor to teach the children of America's heroes each and every day."*

*- Angela Wilson*

As a teacher for the United States Department of Defense Education Activity who teaches military students domestically and abroad, it is no surprise that Angela Wilson chose her own quote. "Educating the children of America's heroes is truly an honor," states Angela. "While everyone supports the troops...there are also family members and children. They are heroes too, and sacrifice quite a bit." Many children of military personnel live in foreign countries, sometimes moving 10 to 14 times before they graduate from high school. Angela gets a little teary-eyed speaking about her students. She says, "They don't even know how amazing they are…how strong, resilient, and perfect examples they are of courage and perseverance.…So, it's my honor to teach them."

While military students are like regular kids in many ways, Angela points out some key differences. Most notably, they move all the time. It is also not unusual for parents to be deployed five times or more. Therefore, birthdays are commonly celebrated without at least one parent. Another difference is that her students possess vast world and cultural experiences due to the places they have lived and visited. Angela recognizes, "This makes them enormously well-balanced and global in perspective." So, no matter where Angela is, she loves to share her quote to "bring awareness and highlight the honor it is to teach the children of America's heroes."

**Background**

Angela Wilson comes from a big family of educators. Her father is a college professor and her mother is a Head Start director. Angela's husband is a teacher and so are her two sisters. Teaching, it could be said, is in the family's blood. While that may be true, Angela remembers a pivotal point in her life that made her want to become a teacher.

As a young person, Angela lived in the South Pacific Island of Tonga. When her family moved back to the United States mainland, Angela entered kindergarten. As a student, she was shy and insecure. Angela remembers, "I felt lost and alone in class." Interestingly enough, Angela's kindergarten teacher never made an attempt to connect with her. Oftentimes, Angela recounts being in the corner of the room, feeling invisible. Two months into the school year, Angela's teacher asked her mother if Angela was deaf, because she never spoke. Needless to say, Angela's mom was shocked. Kindergarten was a completely lost year.

In first grade, Angela's experience was remarkably different and extremely positive. From the very beginning, Mrs. Barbara Ure, her teacher, made a clear effort to know Angela. "Mrs. Ure got down on her knees, looked me in the eyes, and asked, 'What is your name and what do you like to do?'" recalls Angela. When Mrs. Ure discovered that Angela loved to draw, she gave her plenty of opportunities to practice. In fact, Angela fondly remembers winning first place in an all-school art competition that slowly built her confidence. Mrs. Ure was not an ordinary teacher. She would call home to check-in when Angela was absent. She would also come to her house to discuss with her mom the social issues Angela was having at school. In addition, Mrs. Ure created special incentives – personalizing and differentiating instruction – to encourage specific behaviors like contributing Angela's voice in class. In summing up her time with Mrs. Ure, Angela shares, "I don't remember learning to read, but I remember that my teacher loved me." It was then, in first grade at the age of six, that Angela knew she wanted to be a teacher. In particular, she wanted to be a teacher like Mrs. Ure.

Angela Wilson has taught in the United States as well as Korea, Turkey, and Italy. In a little over a decade as an educator, she has been recognized by numerous organizations for her exceptional teaching. In 2012, Angela was named the Department of Defense Education Activity Teacher of the Year, National Teacher of the Year

Finalist, and Mediterranean Teacher of the Year. Angela received her bachelor's degree in education with top honors from Western Illinois University. She was also awarded her master's degree in education from Southern Utah University.

**Teacher Top 5**

1. *Build Relationships*: From her own experience as a student and a teacher, teaching is not simply about delivering instruction, covering curriculum, and preparing students for tests. Rather, it is about building strong relationships to educate the whole child. Angela declares, "The only way to know each child is to develop relationships. Some people see this as 'fluff'…but without relationships, lifelong learning cannot take place….Relationships and connections are the single most valuable use of a teacher's time." By building relationships, students feel that they are valued and heard. As a result, Angela exclaims, "They'll exceed your expectations of them every single time."

So how does Angela build relationships? There are three steps. First, it is vitally important to know each student not only academically, but also personally. Student interests, personal goals, biggest fears, and idiosyncrasies all fall into the personal attribute category. Next, the first homework assignment is actually for the parents. As an 'informative assessment,' parents are asked to write about their child in one million words or less. This provides Angela a tremendous amount of information to who the child is from a parent perspective. Lastly, Angela conducts plenty of "Get to Know You" activities. This is then followed up throughout the year with active listening, deep discussions, and collaboration.

2. _Only So Many Tomorrows_: As a little girl, Angela watched "Little House on the Prairie," starring Michael Landon. Angela remembers Landon's personal battle with pancreatic cancer. In an interview, Landon stated, "Live life to the fullest – each and every day. Whatever you want to do, do it today. There are only so many tomorrows." As an educator who teaches military children, it is not unusual for Angela to attend a memorial service for one of her student's parents. For this reason and many more, Landon's words resonate. Angela testifies, "We never know where life will take us. Savor each day and seize the moment. Live each day as if it is your last."

In teaching children, it means making certain that every lesson is the most effective and creative way to reach students. All too often, students do not remember what was taught, because teachers do not connect the students with the content. Angela explains, "We need to make sure what we're doing with skills and standards are memorable. Memorable moments come from dynamic differentiation, hands-on learning, critical thinking, collaboration, and discussion." She encourages teachers to reexamine outdated lessons and think deliberately about how best to maximize the efficacy of instructional time with students. After all, there are only so many tomorrows.

3. _Create Memorable Moments_: Angela believes, "Life is all about creating memorable moments…moments that won't be forgotten tomorrow, next year, or even next decade." That is one of the keys for successful teaching. How does a teacher create these moments? "Memorable moments are created by connections and experiences that involve multiple senses," asserts Angela.

As an example, Angela discusses a project-based lesson called "Grammar Idol – the Eight Parts of Speech," which was student-generated and teacher-guided. Recognizing that students retain concepts best when they are able to teach someone else the same material, students were tasked with creating and performing a song in order to teach others about their respective teacher-given group's part of speech. Students wrote original lyrics, created band names, made posters, and even developed a rubric. There were preliminary tryouts, and then finalists performed for the entire middle school. Trophies and certificates were awarded. Best yet, Grammar Idol CDs were burned and given out. Grammar Idol even toured, going to the elementary school, to perform. In the end, it was a successful and memorable moment. Angela states, "I could have given them a [grammar] worksheet, but this is what we should be doing, listening to students and basing activities on interests that are current." She adds, "We don't want our memories to be a blank slate."

4. *Assume Nothing*: This is one of Angela's most important mantras. She comments, "It [is] a constant reminder that we never know the circumstances, background, or emotions someone else is bringing to the table." It is especially true when working with middle school and military students. Middle school is an exploratory time and students should be encouraged to find their strengths. More so, military students have experiences that are enormously varied, so assumptions should not be made.

When she was in high school, Angela was enormously shy, but her teacher asked her to participate on the debate team. After weeks of continued persuasion and encouragement, Angela agreed. To her delight, Angela loved debate and it changed her life, resulting in renewed confidence and a scholarship to college. Angela affirms, "As teachers, we often see something in students that they don't see in themselves." That is why labels on kids should be avoided. When assumptions are made, Angela believes, "It stops the lifelong learning process, and closes doors and opportunities."

5. _Develop Perseverance_: "Military children are some of the most courageous, brave, and strong students I have had the honor to teach. No matter what circumstances they face, they persevere with confidence and zeal," says Angela. Angela believes that teachers can learn from their students. In her case, many of them have more life experiences than the average teacher. Angela states, "We shouldn't be afraid to ask them to share." By doing so, it will be a richer environment for everyone. Teachers are facilitators. Gone are the days when the teacher acted as a sole director. Angela offers, "Allow students to be teachers and leaders in the room." Students are a great resource.

**Other Interview Questions**
_1. Who is/are your role model(s) from an educational perspective?_

Angela's father has always been her biggest role model. As a lifelong educator and professor himself, Angela remembers all the old books her father would always bring home. He, in fact, even made Angela a chalkboard when she was a little girl. Education was always at the forefront. She shares, "My father…instilled a love for learning in me from a young age….I have watched him as teacher, administrator, and chair/dean at university education programs. His work ethic is unmatched and his example and advice on education have been my guide."

*2. When you take a look at teachers, in general, and recognize all the hard work and devotion they put into their jobs, what would you say is the one thing that you think teachers can improve upon so they can become more highly effective?*

"Speak up! Teacher voice is missing in education in general," exclaims Angela. As a National Teacher of the Year finalist, it has been an eye-opening experience. Many decisions and initiatives made in education, whether it is at the federal, state, or local level, are done so with little or no teacher input. Angela asserts, "Teachers should be the majority, not the minority....Teachers are on the ground level and know what works and what doesn't." Teachers are an untapped resource. Angela states, "Our voice should be the deciding factor in major decisions regarding education." She continues, "As teachers, we need to advocate for teacher voice."

*3. Are there policies that your school (or past school) has adopted which allow teachers to excel?*

A while ago, Angela moved from her elementary school to a brand new middle school. She served as the Co-Chair for Continuous Improvement, helping lead the development of the school. One of the things they did right was create an environment of collaboration, involving all stakeholders such as teachers, students, parents, and community members. Angela states, "We did a good job...to include the teacher's voice which is often lost in education...we got teachers involved in a lot of big decisions." Those decisions included creating a vision for the school from mission statement to mascot. Interestingly enough, Angela notes that students also helped in crafting the mission and selecting the mascot. Just like coming up with classroom rules, Angela knows, "Students buy into the rules, because they helped create them." In other words, people are more likely to support a world that they help build. That's what Angela and her school have done.

*4. In order to improve our educational system, what are the shortcomings you notice in schools. What are some of the good things happening? What do you think needs to change?*

With school budget cuts, Angela points out that professional development for teachers is nearly non-existent. From conversations with other educators, Angela articulates that ongoing professional development, embedded as part of the job, is the number one want and need. She advocates for professional development that "is not a shot in the dark, but something related to what they're teaching…to perfect their craft or assist in differentiation." In the classroom, teachers guide and mentor students on an ongoing basis, helping them set and reach goals. Angela believes teachers should be treated no differently. Teachers need to set personal and professional goals with the guidance of caring administrators. Quality and continuous professional development, embedded into the job, would go a long way to help accomplish this.

# CHAPTER 8

**Alex Kajitani**
National Teacher of the Year Finalist (2009)
(Math – Grade 8)

*"That which we are, we shall teach, not voluntarily, but involuntarily."*
— *Ralph Waldo Emerson*

In 1841, Ralph Waldo Emerson published the essay, "The Over-Soul," which included the line above. Almost 175 years later, Alex Kajitani selected this as his favorite education quote. Alex shares that this is the simple realization of teaching. He states, "Whoever we are, is what we end up teaching our students."

Educators have a unique opportunity to stand in front of children every day and share who they are as a person. Alex knows that the character and personality of the teacher set the tone for the classroom. Alex explains that if a teacher is ethical, then the modeled behavior will flow to the students in the classroom. Hence, children will learn ethical behavior. If a teacher is calm in demeanor, it will be so in his or her classroom. If a teacher uses eloquent speech on a daily basis, students will listen, learn, and adopt this language as their own. Alex reminds us that teaching is an enormous responsibility, and it is important to remember: who we are, is what we teach.

**Background**

Combine the highest level of innovation with student-centered teaching and the result is Alex Kajitani. He is truly a hands-on educator with real world experiences. Prior to becoming a full-time teacher, Alex traveled the world surfing in exotic locations and operated a thriving restaurant in Santa Barbara. Alex comments, "I wanted to be a teacher who traveled so I could share the world with my students, and I wanted to be a teacher with some business experience so I could tell them about the world and requirements for working in the world."

One of Alex's key secrets for successful teaching is identifying what works best for his students and putting a plan into action. When Alex initially began his teaching career, he worked with young people in one of San Diego's poorest neighborhoods. Issues of poverty, racism, and gang recruitment were rampant. Students were disengaged and did not have a connection with school. That said, Alex states, "[E]very day those students walk into my classroom with the same hopes and dreams as so many other 13-year-olds, to learn, to grow, and to connect with other human beings."

What Alex observed, in particular, was his students' love of music, rap music. The songs, unfortunately, glorified drugs and violence, and exploited women. To connect students' interest to what he was teaching, Alex developed rap songs focused specifically on math. With no background in playing an instrument or even singing karaoke, Alex wrote lyrics and added lines about making good decisions and leading healthy lifestyles. As it would go, students not only embraced Alex's mathematical raps, but they also began to excel academically. On assessments, student performance rose like a rocket. From there, it is all history, and "The Rappin' Mathematician" was born. Alex went on to create CDs and workbooks that are used in thousands of homes and classrooms, and are available at www.MathRaps.com.

Throughout his teaching career, Alex Kajitani has always been able to find that little something that connects him with his students. In his Council of Chief State School Officers' Teacher of the Year video, Alex declares, "I teach because it's an opportunity to live forever. Beauty fades, money runs out, machines fall apart. Our ideas are the only true possessions that can be passed down from one generation to the next." For his creativity and strength in his teaching, Alex has been recognized by countless organizations. He was named California State Teacher of the Year and National Teacher of the Year Finalist in 2009. He was also the National Winner of the "Making a Difference" Award and his students won the "Innovative Video in Education" Award when they made a rap video out of one of his rap songs.

Alex holds a bachelor's degree in sociology, and master's degree in curriculum and instruction from San Diego State University.

**Teacher Top 5**

1. _Be Real_: This is the core tenet of Alex's teaching philosophy and is broken down into three levels. First, it's vital to "Be Relevant." Students need to know that what they are learning is relevant to their everyday lives. Therefore, making connections is imperative. Secondly, teachers must "Be Reliable." This includes starting class on time as well as running it efficiently and in an organized manner. Alex emphasizes, "Demand from students what YOU are." Lastly, all teachers must "Be Realistic." While many people may desire students to pursue traditional careers, educators must have a greater understanding of their students. Alex says, "Perhaps not everyone of my students is going to be a doctor, a lawyer, or even go to college, but everyone of them is going to be a co-worker, a neighbor, and a friend." Realistic expectations must exist and students ought to be accepted for who they are, while continuing to push toward who they can become. Alex adds, "[E]ducators can invoke in our students compassion, equity, and the determination of a better world." That is the crux of a teacher's responsibility.

2. _Every Failure Is Opportunity for Success_: Teachers not only deliver curriculum, but also problem solve. In fact, Alex states, "Sometimes, innovation is finding solutions to problems." That is how Alex took a chance and bridged math instruction with rap music. The first time Alex rapped his math songs in front of students, they laughed. Needless to say, Alex was dejected and disappointed. What seemed like an abject failure, however, was actually a tremendous success. Later that day, when Alex walked into the lunchroom, he observed

that students were rapping his songs. Wow! Over the next few days, Alex noticed a heightened level of enthusiasm among his students. They were excited to come to math class, and it was quite apparent that Alex had figured out what resonated with his students.

In evaluating the effectiveness of his risk-taking, Alex practices self-reflection. He states, "You must hold yourself accountable… what worked and what didn't.…Self-reflection is about being honest with yourself." While coming up with rap songs taps into Multiple Intelligences Theory and culturally relevant pedagogy, part of the reality is that Alex was simply trying to survive as a teacher in order to reach his students. When an educator can be honest with himself and distill the true issue at hand, only then can progress be made. For Alex, he was able to do all of this, and did it just right.

3. _Provide Culturally Relevant Curriculum to Students_: According to Alex, the best teachers do not simply deliver curriculum and instruction. They get students to talk. Then, teachers listen carefully. Alex comments, "They'll tell you who they are." This way, teachers can make their teaching relevant to whom they are teaching. As a result, students stay engaged in the learning process. Interestingly, Alex asserts, "Education should never be color blind."

A good example is how Alex conducts his algebra class when covering the topic of graphing lines. Instead of using trite inputs for "x" and "y," Alex considers the fact that his student population is largely Hispanic with many newly immigrated. With that in mind, Alex uses subjects such as high school drop-out rates, ethnicity, and gender as his dependent variables. By doing so, students pay extra close attention, because the topic immediately becomes germane.

If educators teach in a way that is culturally relevant, Alex states, "Nothing is more relatable."

4. _The Silent Conspiracy_: One of the most egregious aspects of teaching is allowing certain students to slip through the cracks, because they are quiet in class. Students who do not draw attention to themselves are often at risk. The quiet student regularly does not require much of the teacher. It becomes a reality of no expectations versus setting high or low expectations for others.

Alex recounts an incident a long time ago when he stopped at a traffic light, waiting for pedestrians to cross. He noticed a young pregnant girl. When they locked eyes, Alex remembered that she was a former student from the previous year. Tried as he could, Alex recounts, "I could not remember her name and realized that I knew nothing about her." The reason, of course, is that this former student sat quietly in class. This epiphany was a hard-learned lesson. From then on, Alex vowed to never let any child slip through the cracks due to a taciturn demeanor.

5. _Act Like It's Cool and It Will Become Cool_: How do you promote good decisions and attitudes? Alex does it by stopping to figure out how to connect with his students. He also adds a little flair from his own personality. In his classroom, he lauds the term, "Kajitani-style," on students who are doing something positive. For instance, homework that is formatted correctly is extolled as "Kajitani-style." At the same time, "Kajitani-style" can also be a compliment like a student's new haircut. Alex states, "'Kajitani-style' becomes the culture of the classroom." In fact, it can also lead to endorsements by Alex. If a student (e.g., Jose Lopez) demonstrates a noteworthy behavior, Alex

may call it "Lopez-style." The intent is to identify positive student qualities and treat them as praiseworthy. In doing so, Alex believes that he is teaching kids to have pride in themselves. As he maintains, "Every teacher can do this and make it unique. Older kids may need more convincing, but that's when they need it most."

## Other Interview Questions

*1. Who is/are your role model(s) from an educational perspective?*

Alex selects authors Dr. Harry K. Wong and Dr. Paulo Freire as his educational role models.

Dr. Wong wrote *The First Days of School,* a pragmatic and no-nonsense approach about classroom management. Alex asserts, "This [book] is relevant each year you teach, even when you have taught many years." Alex likes the common sense insights about daily routines and how it promotes structure in running an effective class.

Dr. Paulo Freire was a thought leader in education. His *Pedagogy of the Oppressed* helped found the critical pedagogy movement. Prior to entering the teaching profession, Alex read Dr. Freire's work and found it inspirational. Alex recalls, "The recognition that poor people needed to be empowered via education was a simple truth." As a matter of fact, the more oppressed one is, the more education that is needed. This philosophy resonated with Alex and helped shape his educational philosophy.

*2. When you take a look at teachers, in general, and recognize all the hard work and devotion they put into their jobs, what would you say is the one thing that you think teachers can improve upon so they can become more highly effective?*

Alex reiterates the importance of bringing real world relevance to curriculum. He states, "Students should never leave a classroom wondering, 'Why did we learn what we learned?' Teachers must stop and ask, 'Why do students need to know this?'" If educators can answer this effectively and show students the significance in their own lives, then teachers will be successful.

*3. Are there policies that your school (or past school) has adopted which allow teachers to excel?*

Alex remarks that smaller professional learning communities have encouraged collaboration among teachers, relieved isolation, and elevated instruction. At his school, there are approximately 400 students per grade level. By splitting the students into four groups of 100 and designating five teachers to instruct math, science, and so forth, students learn in a more personal environment. Alex says, "Teachers can provide laser-like focus for students' needs." In addition, teachers can plan inter-disciplinary curriculum with impact.

At his school, the informal "Free Lunch for Subs Program" is another policy that has been successful. In economically-challenged schools, it is often difficult to attract good teachers, especially substitute teachers. What did Alex's school do? They partnered teachers with substitute teachers. Alex explains, "At lunch, the collaborating teacher would introduce himself or herself, offer a free lunch coupon, and invite the substitute to sit with him or her at a table." While this effort to promote collegiality among educators seemed small, its impact was huge. Over time, the institution gained a reputation where high quality substitute teachers all wanted to teach due to its warm and welcoming environment.

*4. In order to improve our educational system, what are the shortcomings you notice in schools. What are some of the good things happening? What do you think needs to change?*

As some of the obvious shortcomings, Alex identifies the overemphasis on standards-based testing and near elimination of the arts and physical education due to budgetary constraints. Alex declares, "We are not educating the whole child." In addition, the public perception of teachers also needs to be improved. He believes that there are some really incredible educators in schools who are doing amazing things. This needs to be highlighted. In parallel, teacher evaluations must be robust and encourage self-reflection. When a teacher is not performing satisfactorily, the evaluation system must offer those individuals the ability, whatever it may be, to change.

There are many good things happening in schools. "The movement to professional learning communities is a positive step," says Alex. The mainstreaming of students with special needs has also been constructive – more inclusion and receiving of services and emotional support in the general education classroom benefit those with needs without being ostracized. In terms of food on campus, the focus on healthy alternatives and elimination of junk foods has been good. Lastly, Alex points out, "This interview of 'What a highly effective teacher is?' can only help our educational community."

# CHAPTER 9

## Wilma Ortiz
Massachusetts State Teacher of the Year (2011)
(English Language Learner – Grades 7 to 8)

*"Be the change you want to see in the world."*
*"Live as if you were to die tomorrow. Learn as if you were to live forever."*
— *Mahatma Ghandi*

Like many teachers, Wilma Ortiz's plate is very full with duties and responsibilities pulling her in every direction. Aside from teaching, Wilma is also involved in a number of educational projects, adding additional pressure and time constraints. Ghandi's quotes remind her to slow down and think, reflect, and learn. She states, "These two quotes have been my compass in life to analyze where I am, where

I want to be, and to slow down." By adopting these quotes in her own professional life, Wilma says, "It allows me to be critical of what I do."

In her classroom, Wilma showcases Ghandi's quotes front and center, right underneath her bulletin board. At the beginning of the academic year, she talks with students about what type of year to expect; what will be accomplished; and how important it is to keep learning and living up to our potential. During the year, Wilma shares the importance of self-reflection. She adds, "There are moments where we have to slow down, think and question…what we're doing." Reflection is imperative for everyone.

## Background

As a young person growing up in Puerto Rico, Wilma was surrounded by teachers in her family. Her mother taught science and her relatives were instructors in math, social studies, Spanish, and music. Wilma claims, "I was born to be a teacher." Since there were so many educators in her family circle, she shares, "It shaped me in choosing the profession as a way of connecting with people and trying to see the change I wanted to see in the world."

When she was a little girl, Wilma remembers playing classroom teacher with her dolls. She would line them up, teach a myriad of lessons from math to science, provide breaks and snack time, and give assignments. Wilma says, "Playing classroom teacher…I think that was my way of enacting what was inside and embodying the teacher in me."

Wilma has come a long way since her doll-playing days. She is recognized nationally as an outstanding English language learner educator. She has also demonstrated a long-standing commitment to culturally responsive teaching and incorporates a strong social justice perspective in her classroom. In 2011, Wilma was selected as Massachusetts State Teacher of the Year. Among her many recognitions, she also received the Latino Educational Excellence Award and was the recipient of the Antonia Pantoja Award for leadership and service to the community. In addition to teaching English language learners, Wilma serves as Clinical Faculty for University of Massachusetts School of Education and provides professional development through the Western Massachusetts Writing Project ("WMWP"). After twenty-three years of teaching English language learners at the secondary level, Wilma joined the faculty at Westfield State University School of Education as a full-time Assistant Professor, while she continues her leadership in the WMWP with the new English language learner educational state reform.

Wilma received her bachelor's degree in secondary education from the University of Puerto Rico. She also holds a master's degree in bilingual education and English language acquisition, and a doctoral degree in language literacy and culture from the University of Massachusetts, Amherst.

## Teacher Top 5

1. *Get to Know Your Students and Their Worlds*: If students do not connect with their teachers, Wilma believes that the curriculum of any course will not make sense. She states, "Learning is about relationships and interactions with 'texts.'" Humans, in this case, are the texts. Wilma continues, "We embody the world....As we engage

with each other, and get to know each other, we learn to interact with written and academic texts." This student-teacher connection is critical, especially when teachers hold influence in the classroom. Wilma comments, "We transmit our passion and love for learning. Students have to feel that way [too] and it happens in connection with the adults." That is why the teacher must make a tremendous effort to get to know everyone.

To build relationships, there are plenty of activities by which to do so, including basic data gathering techniques via questionnaires as well as student and teacher shares. In her class, Wilma enjoys performing an activity called Free Topic which is done once per week. Here, students talk to each other and communicate with the class what they did over the weekend. Wilma states, "You'd be surprised how revealing it is." She also tasks students with personal narrative writing which often uncovers personal values, beliefs, experiences, and things that are closest to their hearts.

2. _Reflection as Praxis is as a Habit of Mind_: Paulo Freire was one of the great educational minds who influenced Wilma's own teaching. She declares, "A teacher that reflects critically is not afraid of making mistakes...I see those moments as transformative, if we humbly understand that mistakes are a way of learning, and helping us get where we want to go." Therefore, self-reflection must be practiced routinely. Mistakes should be seen as a stepping stone to get to the next level.

All too often, student achievement is based on feedback, and many times, it is negative. Wilma sees the idea of "if you're not correct, you fail," as a serious detriment and impediment to learning. She states, "We have to re-think and re-define mistakes as a positive way of learning and reflect on what we're doing." In her own classroom, Wilma pushes students to reflect critically and deeply. For instance, student writing is evaluated by posing questions and surfacing counter-arguments, without casting judgment.

3. _Maintain Communication With Your Students' Parents or Guardians_: Having parents feel like they are a part of their child's learning process is vital. Wilma asserts, "It's so important in the equation of academic success." According to Wilma, teachers need to "promote, encourage, and provide opportunities for parent/ guardian involvement and engagement." At the same time, educators must realize that many parents have non-traditional schedules and may not be able to avail themselves to traditional school events such as open houses and parent-teacher conferences. In these cases, Wilma recommends thinking outside-of-the-box. At her previous school, Wilma remembers her English language leaner department scheduling meetings with parents on Sundays at the town library. It was an accommodation for parents who were only available then. In all of this, the key is to make sure teachers understand their students' home life via a strong parent-teacher partnership.

4. _Be an Advocate for Students, Parents and Colleagues_: When school practices disadvantage certain segments of the population, Wilma suggests asking questions and challenging the status quo. A prime example is when a school offers a new program, but the information is not communicated or translated to the entire community. In many instances, English language learner students and parents are left out, which reveals the inequity at schools.

To become an advocate for others, Wilma believes that teachers must get involved. Schools have different governances and counsels such as leadership committees and curriculum coordinators. Teachers should seek out these positions and become advocates and activists. Another way is through community organizations. Wilma regularly reaches out to universities in her area to learn about what types of programs they have. In the past, she brought to her school volunteer tutors for her after-school clubs. She also got developed a close relationship with the "school to career" organizer. Wilma states, "I volunteer and become a member of different programs so I can help my English language learner students and make opportunities available to them."

5. _Make the Curriculum Relevant and Applicable_: In order to teach the skills and content required by national and state standards, Wilma connects the aforementioned to the students' worlds, making it relevant. She utilizes "an inquiry approach to learning, becoming a partner in the learning process along with her students." Wilma makes connections at the micro-level, by beginning with school life topics. She then gradually opens up to the community and town. The ultimate goal is to transition students to a macro-perspective, involving the entire world. Wilma articulates, "It's bringing students' interests in as a hook, so they make the applications of their learning relevant."

For example, Wilma's eighth grade class covered the topic of immigration. She asks, "How do we bring in the lives of the students and parents as resources for that unit? What are the common experiences of people coming from another country?" To answer these questions, Wilma asked students to interview their parents/guardians as well as community members. The intent is to broaden the topic beyond the experiences of a particular group, transcending barriers of immigration and finding common threads. Wilma then tasked students to write, create storyboards, and finally publish a storybook.

**Other Interview Questions**

*1. Who is/are your role-model(s) from an educational perspective?*

Wilma comes from a family of teachers, especially from her mother's side. Through the stories they would share and the compassion for their students, Wilma's teacher-relatives were her very first role models. Wilma proclaims, "Their passion for the students, in particular, and the profession, in general, sparked in me a genuine interest in emulating the way they touched so many lives." She continues, "In addition, my own educational experience under the Dominican Nuns' tutelage instilled in me an incredible inspiration in the profession. Their teaching was filled with love, compassion, empathy, and a sense of social justice." While growing up under very modest circumstances, Wilma recalls the nuns helping fund her and her sisters' tuition by awarding "an unheard of scholarship that we won." Later in college, Wilma was influenced by Paulo Freire's pedagogy and principles of education, power, and liberation.

*2. When you take a look at teachers, in general, and recognize all the hard work and devotion they put into their jobs, what would you say is the one thing that you think teachers can improve upon so they can become more highly effective?*

Wilma does not like to generalize and can only speak from her own experience at the secondary level. She states, "[I]t's critical for teachers to find better ways to incorporate the students' background experiences, cultures, and literacies into their lessons/classroom, to build on these agencies, and provide opportunities for exploring and expanding individual potentials. Oftentimes, students disconnect from school and learning when they do not see themselves in the curriculum, or do not see the relevance of what they are learning in their own life." In order to accomplish this, Wilma suggests "[C]areful lesson planning along with knowing the students really well. [This will] allow for making critical spaces available for these types of connections and interactions."

*3. Are there policies that your school (or past school) has adopted which allow teachers to excel?*

According to Wilma, there are many leadership opportunities which allow teachers to participate in a variety of contexts and roles as they see themselves fit. This includes curriculum leaders, leadership committees, student council advisors, and the school improvement council. More specifically, Wilma's middle school established common planning time for teachers to work collaboratively. In fact, Wilma's school district "initiated instructional rounds that provide faculty and staff with opportunities to learn from each other with the intent of improving teaching and learning." This model was derived from the medical field whereby physicians learn from other physicians.

One item to note, however, is that many of these initiatives in schools exist only as long as the monies are available. Wilma states, "[T]hese philosophical practices do not last unless the school creates an infrastructure for long term sustainability." Adopting short-term fixes to remediate issues are not the solution. Rather, she calls these "the bandage approach."

*4. In order to improve our educational system, what are the shortcomings you notice in schools. What are some of the good things happening? What do you think needs to change?*

Wilma identifies structural issues within the educational system that have come short. On a micro-level, there are nominal resources for English language learner teachers. Many times, the teacher is pulled in all directions such as translating for the school nurse when students are ill; assisting the dean's office when an English language learner student has problems; and meeting with the guidance counselors to help address an English language learner student and his or her family. On a macro-level, Wilma comments, "Many of the new education reforms and initiatives continue to put high pressure on teachers to solve all the problems in the students' life…and the malfunction of the educational system…we insist on closing the achievement gap solely from the classroom context [and] we neglect to address and recognize major factors that create this gap." These factors include poverty, health, and societal issues. She continues, "If we continue to focus on standardized assessment as a tool to determine success, the gap will never close. We need to implement a more holistic approach to improve education and avoid placing all the responsibilities on teachers."

As for good things happening, Wilma points to the forthcoming teacher evaluation system. She states, "I see the new teacher evaluation system as an opportunity for teachers to take a more proactive role in their own evaluations. This could be empowering, if administrators create genuine collaborative partnerships with teachers, from the process of figuring out all the details in this new mandate to the planning and implementation of a system that is applicable [to its stated objectives]...."

From Wilma's perspective, there are a number of items that need to be changed. Here are some that she has identified:

- Improve communication between the central office, principals, and teachers. Most decisions are made at the higher level of the institution. Oftentimes, teachers are the last ones to be informed of many decisions that were made without any teacher input. The top down decision-making process needs to change and include the teacher's voice who is on the front lines.

- Place less emphasis on scores and standardized exams and put more effort into creating multiple types of assessments that are formative and summative.

- Re-define family engagement and provide more resources to improve parental support K to 12.

- Re-define standardization. The standardization discourse, unintentionally, is creating a "one-size-fits-all" approach to education. When teachers are expected to teach the same material at the same time, it neglects the individual. Moreover, it dismisses the theoretical framework that considers diversity in the classroom. Therefore, all stakeholders should ask, "Where is the pedagogy for diverse learners and differentiation? Does everyone learn at the same pace and demonstrate learning in equal manner?"

# CHAPTER 10

## Paul Kuhlman
South Dakota State Teacher of the Year (2009)
(Math and Science – Grades 7, 9 to 12)

*"Keep your dreams alive. Understand to achieve anything requires faith and belief in yourself, vision, hard work, determination, and dedication. Remember all things are possible for those who believe."*

— Gail Devers

Dreams are not relegated to Olympians, and a teacher's impact can stick with a student long after he or she graduates. When Paul Kuhlman was asked to write a "Teacher Tale" for the *Chicken Soup for the Soul* series of books, he wrote about "The Power of Belief." His story recounts an email that he received from a former student who credits Paul for his belief in her.

She writes, "I needed to tell you that even though we never really talked…you had a big influence on me.…One thing I always remembered was a time when you were asking us what we wanted to do when we grew up. When my turn came, I said I wanted to be a physicist. Everyone laughed, even me. But you didn't. You said I could be a physicist if I wanted and you were serious. It stayed with me.…"

Paul's positive attitude and unequivocal faith in youth allow his students to believe in themselves, even before they do. That is why Paul chose Gail Devers' quote. It epitomizes the realization of dreams through self-belief and tireless effort. From his "Teacher Tale," Paul writes, "This story illustrates how the greatest strength of a teacher may be the ability to raise the expectations of their students and to convey a personal belief that with hard work, all students can succeed in life. The power of belief in oneself is a truly remarkable gift that should be given to all children. As teachers, we have the ability, and the responsibility, to give this gift to our students!"

**Background**

Like many others, Paul Kuhlman did not plan on becoming a teacher. After coaching a youth baseball team, however, Paul liked the experience so much that he pursued teaching as a full-time profession. He states, "I…found it a very enjoyable experience. This helped lead me to a teaching career. Once I taught a few sample lessons in my first education classes, I knew teaching was something I really wanted to do." The teaching bug had bitten.

Fast-forward and Paul is deep into his 25ᵗʰ year of teaching with no end in sight. He is an accomplished science educator, known for his rigor, fun, and off-the-wall lessons. Paul is also one of the most heavily sought after teachers by students. One student said, "I think I've taken every one [class] he offers. It doesn't matter what it is, if he's teaching. I take it." In his students' eyes, having Paul as a teacher is definitely worth the hard work. Perhaps that is because the line between learning and fun is completely blurred in his classroom. Activities and experiments are often thrilling. Paul is very deliberate and finds the most exciting way to give demonstrations, adding a bit of flair and an appearance of danger. "I just like having fun in the classroom…in this day and age, we try to have a little excitement in the class," says Paul. Everything studied relates to the real world so that students can understand. Most importantly, Paul loves what he does and students feed off of him. Paul states, "When I come to school, it's not work. It's play time for me. Ninety percent of my day is fun. It's all about the kids in the long run."

For all of his outstanding work, Paul has been recognized by numerous organizations. He was given the Presidential Award for Excellence in Mathematics and Science Teaching in 2011. He was named the 2009 South Dakota State Teacher of the Year. He was also selected as the 2008 South Dakota Outstanding Physical Science Teacher.

At his school, Paul teaches math, chemistry, and physics. He also served as a consultant to the South Dakota Department of Education and the University of South Dakota's School of Education. In the past, he has taught summer courses at the University of South Dakota.

Paul is a graduate of North Dakota State University with a bachelor's degree in biology. He also holds two master's degrees in secondary administration and natural science from the University of South Dakota.

## Teacher Top 5

1. _Have Passion and Love What You Do_: At the 2009 Teacher of the Year conference, Paul and his recipients were asked to provide a word to describe the attributes of a good teacher. Paul wrote down the word, "passion." Interestingly enough, passion was the number one word chosen by him and his colleagues. Paul says, "I don't know how to define it, but I know it when I see it. It's not just liking kids. It's about liking your kids liking your subject, and wanting to make the connection to your students about your subject." Paul adds that students know if a teacher honestly enjoys teaching or whether he or she is faking it. He states, "They'll know if you say, 'I like math,' but deep down you really don't like it. You're just doing it for the job. They'll figure it out." On the other hand, if students see their teacher working on the subject-matter outside of the classroom during his or her free time, then teacher interest is sincere.

As for passion in teaching, many say that it is inherent in the person. Paul, however, believes that it can be learned over time. "If you're around it enough, it'll rub off. That's why the school culture is really important when you build a staff," declares Paul. Either way, students know when they have struck gold and have a great teacher. In the classroom, students feel special, and they know that the subject is special too.

2. _Embrace the Love of Learning_: If educators want to instill the belief that learning is important, then teachers must follow that lead. Paul emphatically stresses, "Continued education is a necessity! Your kids need to see that you are an active participant in the learning process." In delivering instruction, teachers should never be satisfied with their lessons. They should always be seeking ways to make it better in order to reach different kinds of learners.

Continuing education exists in a variety of forms. Paul strongly suggests attending professional development that is teacher-led. There is a big difference between a teacher who is practicing what he or she preaches versus someone who is removed from the classroom. Paul also recommends, "Anything that includes collaboration between teachers. Sometimes, you learn as much from people around you as you do from the instructor." If Paul could have it his way, he would love to have a continuing education roundtable once a month with science teachers in his district. This way, teachers could share ideas and discuss learning techniques that have worked.

3. _Dedicate Yourself_: As a dedicated teacher, it is inevitable that there will be things given up in his or her personal life in order to make the learning experience the best it can be in the classroom. While sacrifice exists in most occupations requiring excellence, teachers must accept this as a fact. Paul exclaims, "What teachers do is extremely important! Don't underestimate the influence that you can have on a child. Think about that every time you enter your classroom. You only get that child for one year. What will you do for them?"

Like many teachers, Paul points out an obvious truism. He states, "It's amazing how many times you're out [of the classroom], but thinking about the school." If that happens, there is a good chance that dedication runs in your veins. It is the little things that make the difference. Maybe it is spending an extra ten minutes to hone a lesson or perform a first-time demonstration that requires extra prep work. Either way, Paul encourages teachers to go for it and be the best they can be.

4. _Listen! Your Kids Know A Lot!_: For a teacher, listening is just as important as teaching itself, if not more so. Paul says, "Listen… they'll lead you to where you have to go." Sometimes, the task of the teacher will be to clarify misconceptions. In Paul's experience, this happens quite a bit in science. For example, do heavier objects fall faster than lighter ones? The answer begins by starting with what students know. Other times, students add considerable value. "Take advantage of the experiences they bring into the classroom," says Paul. Many students possess a wealth of knowledge and simply need the encouragement to share their voice.

If the student-teacher rapport is strong, Paul believes, "Students will tell you a lot about yourself…if you are being too hard or too soft, too judgmental, or in a bad mood. They'll let you know." Listening is all about giving students respect and taking the time to know students well.

5. _Practice the Golden Rule_: One should treat others as one would like to be treated. This maxim is not just empty talk. The classroom must be a safe, enjoyable place for learning. He states, "You want your classroom to be a happy place. I want my kids to be happy. I want to be happy when I'm in there." Laughter, smiles, high fives, or whatever it may be, it all begins with treating each other with

respect. Students need to know what type of behavior is acceptable. Classroom rules help. However, modeling is the best antidote. Paul comments, "Be consistent…realize that some things are little things so it doesn't disrupt learning." If a student does not have a pencil every day, it is not the end of the world. Come up with a positive solution to remedy the situation. "Don't make little disruptions into big disruptions," says Paul.

**Other Interview Questions**

*1. Who is/are your role model(s) from an educational perspective?*

"I don't have a single role model, but I try to take some of the best traits from some of my past teachers," answers Paul. Those educators include his high school science, business, and history teachers.

Paul remembers his science teacher, because the class was always an enjoyable place to be. They performed many experiments and learned new things. Paul says, "I felt like when I went into that class, I learned something."

Mrs. Schultz, Paul's business teacher, comes to mind for her no non-sense style and strong classroom management skills. He recalls a notorious, school-wide troublemaker who was immediately straightened out by her the first week of school. For the next nine weeks, everything was smooth sailing. The most amazing aspect is that Mrs. Schultz did not hold poor behavior against the student. Paul states, "She was very good about separating behavior from identity. She didn't match those two together." To this day, Paul always tries to remember that when he disciplines. "It's nothing personal against you, it's the choices that you're making," notes Paul.

Lastly, Paul's history teacher, who was a former police officer, taught via storytelling. Paul always loved that aspect of his history class. "I still like that today, when I teach science. I love to add a little bit of history," says Paul.

*2. When you take a look at teachers, in general, and recognize all the hard work and devotion they put into their jobs, what would you say is the one thing that you think teachers can improve upon so they can become more highly effective?*

Paul suggests, "Take as many professional development courses in your subject area as possible. Contact industries in your field to learn what types of skills they are looking for and keep them for reference for your classes. Connect what you are teaching to the real world when possible."

Schools and industry are truly symbiotic. Paul has found that companies are more than willing to help. It can take the form of answering questions by industry experts, providing resources like mice or equipment, or performing free water sampling tests. Corporations want students to develop an interest in their field so they can breed talent as future hires. In contacting organizations, Paul recommends directing inquiries to specific departments. He advises, "The closer you get to the source, the better chance you will get a reply."

*3. Are there policies that your school (or past school) has adopted which allow teachers to excel?*

Teaching at a small school – about 262 students K to 12 – has its benefits. Paul declares, "There is a lot of flexibility and freedom, but also more responsibility." When it comes to field trips, for instance, Paul can still get his class to go, even when school budgets have shrunk. That said, requests have to be well thought out and make sense. Paul also points out that teachers have the freedom to try different types of labs. For example, to understand the coefficient of friction, Paul sought the assistance of the highway patrol. Paul's class traveled to a block of highway with no traffic. There, the police created a skid. Using physics to analyze the remaining tire mark, the accident investigator showed students how he determined the speed of the vehicle. School administration is supportive of such activities. Lastly, Paul shares, "[The school] allow[s] us to have fundraisers and support[s] us in attending professional development…." To raise money for the science fair, Paul placed an ad in the local newspaper. With a community of 600 people, checks poured in, totaling $3,000. This occurred without having to put on any type of event. Paul rationalizes, "People want to give to something that they see is good…[especially when] kids are learning and having fun."

*4. In order to improve our educational system, what are the shortcomings you notice in schools. What are some of the good things happening? What do you think needs to change?*

Paul addresses four specific areas: the academic school year; recruitment of the best and brightest to teaching; accountability; and replicating best practices.

The agrarian school calendar is outdated. In comparison to other developed countries, students in the United States attend less school. Paul states, "In South Dakota, it's around 170 to 175 days. Some developed countries have about 220 days. It needs to be longer…to cover the amount of information that needs to be learned."

Recruiting high quality candidates into teaching is imperative. Paul suggests, "Identifying students in high school/early college years who appear to be excellent candidates for teaching. Give them experiences early in the classroom so they get 'hooked.'" That's what happened to Paul. After the first lesson he taught as a junior in college, he knew that teaching was for him. "Lots of times in life, little experiences make the difference," says Paul.

While student test scores should not be 100% of a teacher's evaluation, Paul believes, "Realistically, you should have it as a part, because you have to be accountable to what you're doing in the classroom." It can be a student growth model, for instance. The gist is that a metric needs to be devised to make sure students are not failing year after year. Paul is also in favor of student surveys. Outliers can be thrown out, but a student survey measures the climate of a teacher's classroom. Paul asserts, "We all know climate matters."

Lastly, best teaching practices need to be replicated en masse. Paul queries, "We know what good teaching is. Why can't we replicate it on a large scale?" In South Dakota, they adopted Charlotte Danielson's Framework for Teachers, a research-based set of rubrics used to help teachers become more thoughtful practitioners. Paul believes that this is a good beginning to identify effective traits for successful teaching.

# SECONDARY EDUCATION

# CHAPTER 11

## Yung Romano
Alabama State Teacher of the Year (2010)
(Anatomy, Biology, Environmental Science – Grades 9 to 12)

*"To laugh often and much; to win the respect of intelligent people and the affection of children...to leave the world a better place...to know even one life has breathed easier because you have lived. This is to have succeeded."*
— *Ralph Waldo Emerson*

It is no surprise that Yung Romano chose Ralph Waldo Emerson's quote above. Yung's life story as a refugee from the Vietnam War and belief in living a life of purpose parallel Emerson's words. "We are on Earth for a reason...to serve a purpose," says Yung. "Teaching, as a profession, is one of the greatest callings...you have the possibility of affecting many people, but if you can affect one life, then you've truly lived." Yung is a product of the compassionate and caring guidance of her teachers and mentors. They helped in redirecting her life and allowed her to become who she is. "I wouldn't have known what to do if it wasn't for my teachers and mentors who affected me," claims Yung. Striking a healthy balance between fulfilling her sense of purpose and enriching the lives of others is something that Yung has genuinely accomplished.

## Background

Yung Romano epitomizes a war refugee/immigrant success story, and her path to becoming a teacher is the direct result of the challenges she faced. Yung was born in the midst of the Vietnam War. With the fall of Saigon in 1975, Yung and her parents attempted to flee the country for the United States. Among the chaos and turbulence, she was separated from her mother. Fortunately, Yung's aunt and uncle were there. At the time, she was only six years old. After being airlifted out of the ocean by a United States cargo plane to living in a refugee camp in Guam, she was later flown to Hawaii to begin her American journey.

Life in the United States had its challenges, especially when two divergent cultures are shaping and influencing a young person in her early years. At home, Yung's immediate family was traditional and extraordinarily strict. She states, "My relatives did not believe in showing affection or encouragement. I was raised to be a perfect child who was not allowed to share opinions and feelings. My age and my gender silenced my voice and prevented my feelings from being validated." On the other hand, school was a comforting place. Her teachers' care and compassion were a sanctuary. At school, she not only learned and grew, but it was also acceptable to emote. Yung asserts, "The one thing that I will always honor and cherish is that my teachers all loved me and provided me the emotional support that I didn't get at home…they encouraged my opinions and my creativity, and most important of all, they instilled in me the love of learning."

Many years later, through hard work and perseverance, Yung graduated from Auburn University Montgomery with a bachelor's degree in science (magna cum laude) and a master's degree in education. From there, she entered the field of teaching. "It is because of all these wonderful teachers that I decided I would become a teacher in honor of them and their hard work," says Yung.

In less than a decade of teaching, Yung was named the 2010 Alabama State Teacher of the Year. Her determination, commitment, and fortitude to teach, combined with encouraging her students to overcome challenges, are arguably her greatest hallmarks. She is also actively involved in a variety of organizations, including the Bridge Builders program and the Senior Olympics.

**Teacher Top 5**

1. _Be a Role Model for your Students_: Yung is a strong believer that "education can empower others." By acting as a positive role model, teachers have the unique opportunity to influence students so they can visualize, and then fulfill, their potential. In her first year of teaching, Yung recalls a student whom she helped change. Earlier, the student had a reputation for not only being difficult, but also physically destructive. When the student took Yung's science class, something clicked. In her classroom, Yung often shared her own story. She did so to let students know that hardships and adversity

can be overcome. In time, the student started putting forth strong effort and even began to like science. Yung recollects the student saying, "I've always hated science. This is the first year that I like it. And, that's because of you. Everything I do, I do for you. I try hard, study, and try to make good grades." While Yung was flattered, she shared with the student, "Great. But do it for yourself. Don't do things in life for someone else. And, the first thing you need to do is to improve yourself." That resonated.

Talks between teacher and student may seem so simple. However, its lasting impact can be tremendously significant. In high school, especially, Yung believes, "Students need someone to listen. Not belittle. Guide them so they can see there is something else – alternatives – from their current path." In other words, be a caring role model. As for the student who was in her science class, she ended up becoming Yung's lab assistant the following year. She is now attending a major university with aspirations of becoming a mathematician.

2. _Be Knowledgeable_: While teachers are not expected to know everything all of the time, strong subject-matter knowledge of the class taught is absolutely imperative. Yung proclaims, "Students are very astute at picking up when teachers don't know their material." When that does happen, students pounce. Yung states, "I overhear students talk about teachers who don't know their subject matter, much less teach it to them." That immediately adversely affects the credibility of, and level of respect given to, the teacher. Plus, it is enormously difficult to win their respect back.

Yung recommends seeking out resources to improve subject-material mastery, no matter how proficient a teacher. After all, it is a central obligation as an educator. This can take the form of professional development classes, school district workshops, or partnerships with faculty and university professors. Either way, the intent is to improve and augment his or her repertoire, bringing real-life application to the classroom.

3. _Make What You Teach Relevant_: One of the fundamental principles of Yung's teaching approach is to keep her teaching relevant. She states, "Students are forever asking why they have to learn a particular topic in class....If it doesn't make sense..., then it doesn't warrant putting the effort into learning it." That's why teaching must be authentic. Yung relates the concepts studied in class to "normal things that students do in everyday life." For instance, the topic of amino acids is an abstract idea. She shares, "They cannot touch it or see it. But if I ask them to tell me what they like to throw on the barbecue grill in the summer, and [when] they yell out steak or hamburger, it is a good starting point...to learn about amino acids."

For every lesson taught, Yung makes a big effort to create real-world connections. This is especially true for her ninth graders. She notices that these students are very much in their "Why Stage?" Therefore, abstract concepts need to be made concrete. While students may ask, "Why?," Yung attempts to head off any confusion by anticipating questions before the lesson is taught. She preps and reviews rigorously. At the same time, Yung knows that unforeseen questions will always arise. In that case, she relies on her number two _Teacher Top 5_, Be Knowledgeable.

4. _Have Passion for your Subject Matter_: Teaching through your passions has an enormous benefit to students. Most of the time,

teachers will have strong content knowledge in their subject matter, because it is a personal interest. Yung is a great example. She states, "A successful teacher is one who is constantly learning about his or her subject. My students think I am crazy sometimes when I get so excited about something I learned that was groundbreaking in the field of science." The other benefit is that teacher enthusiasm is contagious. When the teacher gets excited, students sense it and they follow their teacher's lead.

As an example, Yung remembers discovering a strange, odoriferous, yet brilliantly vibrant fungus growing in her backyard. She recalls, "I brought the specimen into class and my students shook their heads over my exuberance over this weird specimen." This odd-looking fungus resembled the ugly-version of a jelly donut filled with oozing, smelly slime. Over the next few days, Yung and her students poured over the Internet to try and identify this unusual plant life. It created quite a stir, but students were enthusiastically researching it. In the end, it was identified as a stinkhorn, a foul-smelling fungus that rots wood. Yung shares, "I still have those same students sending me things they have 'discovered,' because they want to share with me the same experiences that I have shared with them."

5. _Don't Be Afraid to Make Mistakes_: Everyone makes mistakes and teachers are no different. It is simply a part of teaching, no matter how prepared. When a mistake is made, however, it is important to own up to it. In her anatomy and physiology class, Yung described an incident when she mispronounced a term that was being studied. She had unknowingly mispronounced this word all day, but something just felt off. When she went home, Yung researched the word. Sure enough, she had made a mistake. The next day, Yung addressed

the issue head-on. She recalls saying, "I'm sorry. I gave you the correct information, but I pronounced it incorrectly." Then, Yung displayed the word phonetically and demonstrated how it was to be properly pronounced. Yung maintains that it is important to model this behavior, so that students know that it is okay to make mistakes. That way, everyone will be willing to lend their voices in class and learn from each other.

## Other Interview Questions

*1. Who is/are your role model(s) from an educational perspective?*

Due to her family dynamics, Yung identifies all of her past teachers and mentors as incredible role models who helped shape who she is today. There was Mrs. Seibers, her fifth grade teacher, who not only talked Yung's guardians into allowing her to participate in a school camping trip, but also helped raise the money for her to go. Her fourth grade science teacher, Mr. Mathews, was a strong, male role model who offered praise, especially for her artistic rendition of a fish. Mrs. Bradshaw, her third grade teacher, took the time and effort to understand her family dynamics. Having learned that Yung's family did not celebrate Christmas, Mrs. Bradshaw let her save her classroom Christmas gift so that Yung could have something to open up at home on Christmas morning. Yung avows, "Each one of my teachers has made a difference in my life, and each one of them helped me to survive my childhood. Most of them never knew how much they helped me, but in my heart I will always remember them."

*2. When you take a look at teachers, in general, and recognize all the hard work and devotion they put into their jobs, what would you say is the one thing that you think teachers can improve upon so they can become more highly effective?*

"The one thing that teachers can improve upon to become more highly effective is to be able to work as one cohesive group on a state and national level to give a teachers' perspective on what makes a successful student and school," states Yung. She adds, "Teachers have to be able to not only voice these thoughts, but also somehow make state and national law-making bodies take heed of these opinions." Yung points out that standardized tests are somewhat disconnected from whom is assessed. Students have many different types of backgrounds. It is perplexing to use a uniform assessment for everyone. Yung states, "Teachers are with students, day in and day out." Hence, the teachers' voice should be part of the decision-making process to determine what makes an educational construct acceptable and successful.

*3. Are there policies that your school (or past school) has adopted which allow teachers to excel?*

Some school districts recognize the value of allowing teachers to teach creatively in order to reach all types of learners. Yung does not believe the one-size-fits-all "cookie cutter model" of scripted lessons works. After all, she states, "Teachers are not cooks following a recipe." In the past, Yung taught at a performing arts magnet school that allowed instructional autonomy. She states, "The staff at the school were amazing and talented artists in their own right, and they were given the freedom to design their curriculum [while meeting state standards] to pass on their knowledge to the students." She continues, "As a core subject teacher at the school, I was able to collaborate with the performing arts teachers to come up with lessons that would bridge the arts with science...[we] would collaborate.... My students learned about the anatomy and physiology of the human bones which helped them sketch and draw in their art class. I don't think there were any formal policies that the school adopted to allow for this partnership, but rather a mentality of the school to work as a cohesive group to provide the most benefit for the students."

*4. In order to improve our educational system, what are the shortcomings you notice in schools? What are some of the good things happening? What do you think needs to change?*

Yung notices that there is a need for collaboration between high schools and universities/colleges to help students connect the knowledge and skills from high school to the next phase of their educational career. This is good, but she also points out that high schools need to recognize that not every student desires to pursue a career that requires a traditional college education. Instead, students have a whole host of vocational aspirations such as automotive machinery, cosmetology, and landscape architecture. In this case, Yung suggests "vocational tracks." "Their curriculum should look different than those who want to go on to higher education. Teachers can become specialized to teach different tracks," says Yung. However, she continues, "All students need to be proficient in reading, writing, and math."

An area that needs higher scrutiny is the selection process for those aspiring to become teachers. Yung declares, "Too many times when I ask pre-service teachers why they want to go into the teaching profession, I get the same answer...I love children. My reply...is that my postman loves children, but he would fail miserably in the classroom."

119

She believes that the selection process for teacher candidates "should not be an 'open-door' policy for anyone to walk into and 'decide' they want to pursue teaching." Rather, she explains, "Courses should be more rigorous in colleges that offer teacher education programs and teacher-candidates should spend more time working in the school sites for the duration of their college career." That way, prospective teacher candidates know what to expect. For those who choose to pursue teaching thereafter, there will be a higher likelihood that they will stay in the profession longer.

# CHAPTER 12

## Leslie Nicholas

NEA Member Benefits Award for Teaching Excellence (2013)
(English, Journalism – Grades 9 to 12)

*"Lilies that fester smell far worse than weeds."*
*— William Shakespeare*

As an English teacher, Les Nicholas loves this quote from Shakespeare's "Sonnet 94." Lilies have the potential to be a beautiful flower. They are a gift and should be truly cherished. However, weeds exist as they are, no matter what the circumstance. Les believes this quote expresses a profound truth relating to students and learning. In his more than 30 years of experience, he has taught many students like lilies who are capable of earning high marks, but they are content with unexceptional performance. At the same time, there are always those students who put forth incredible effort simply to reach a modest mark. Les praises and compliments these learners who give it their all. They are who they are, but their strong work ethic will promote resiliency and benefit them enormously in life. As the great runner Steve Prefontaine stated, "To give anything less than your best is to sacrifice the gift."

## Background

What sets Les Nicholas apart from many educators is his commitment to authentic learning and teaching life skills. How often do students walk to school and state, "I'm going to work" instead of "I'm going to class"? The juxtaposition of interesting work versus boring school, and its relevancy to students, is an educational philosophy that embodies Les and his teaching style. In his journalism class, that is what happened. Les built a radio station and television studio in the classroom where students work on broadcast radio and television shows. It is truly hands-on learning and students love it.

For over 30 years, Les Nicholas has taught English and journalism at Wyoming Valley West High and Middle School. He is a unique teacher who motivates students beyond simply doing well on a pencil and paper test. Rather, Les believes in teaching life skills that are relevant. At his school, Les has served in numerous production and editorial capacities, including broadcast, newspaper, and yearbook. He was also an honor society adviser, track and field coach, and football announcer.

Les has been recognized by numerous organizations and institutions. He was inducted into the National Teachers Hall of Fame in

2009 and named both the University of Pennsylvania Educator of the Year in 2005 and State Teacher of the Year for Pennsylvania in 2004. He also received many awards such as the Horace Mann Award for Teaching Excellence, Great American Teacher Award, First Freedom Award, Wal-Mart Teacher of the Year, and Disney Teacher Award.

Les received his bachelor's in English at Wilkes College and master's at University of Pennsylvania.

## Teacher Top 5

1. *Keep It Real*: Students need to know what they are learning has relevance and practicality in the real world. Otherwise, school can feel disconnected from reality. The best educators teach these life skills without the student ever recognizing that their class work translates into marketable skills well beyond the walls of an academic institution. Les asserts, "The key to teaching creatively and achieving academic results is by combining relevance with rigor. When students recognize they will actually use the material they are studying, motivation becomes self-directed. I strive to provide my students with as many realistic learning experiences as possible, so they see the importance of the skills they learn in the classroom."

To promote authentic learning, Les created a classroom environment that mimics the real world. For his journalism class, he built a radio and television studio. Students broadcast radio and television shows on a closed circuit system. For print media, students publish their writing in the school newspaper and yearbook as well as the local newspaper. Les also adopted the use of podcasts, allowing students to gain a global audience for their writing. According to observers, it was often said that Les' room was "run like a professional newsgathering organization where students went about their business like experts." By doing so, Les "kept it real" and allowed students to buy into their own learning. To sum up, Les quotes William Butler Yeats, "Education is not the filling of a pail, but the lighting of a fire."

2. _The Power of Three_: Part of teacher success is planning appropriately. Les has found that using three activities in a one class period is most effective. Each activity may be divided into varying units of time and some activities are best suited for different ability levels. The important issue is that teachers cannot expect to maintain student attention with one activity for the entire class period. Les states, "You may teach only one concept, but do it in different ways." Moreover, students should never sit idle. There should always be enough engaging material to involve students.

In his journalism class, Les provides the example of story selection. In the first activity, students are introduced to the elements of news, including timeliness, proximity, prominence, consequence, human interest, and conflict. Thereafter, teacher-guided student discussion ensues. For the second activity, a hypothetical news story is presented and students identify news elements displayed on a SmartBoard. In the third activity, a list of ten news stories is exhibited. Groups of four to five students collaborate to select their top five. Using a jigsaw model, each group sends an ambassador to a neighboring group to learn of their choices. Then, the ambassador returns and debriefs with his or her original group. Given the newfound information, group discussions continue with an informed perspective from other groups. In the end, story selection choices and its justification are heard from each group. The class then selects the top five stories which form the basis for homework.

3. _Behaviors Must Be Practices_: In Les' classroom, practicing behaviors is essential to developing compassion and confidence. During the first week of school, team procedures are explained, modeled, and practiced. By doing so, student expectations are set and the classroom can run effectively and efficiently. Les notes several examples, including when it is appropriate to raise hands, the proper way to encourage a classmate, and how students should respond when quieting down. Other housekeeping items, such as passing in homework assignments, picking up journals, and following emergency drill procedures, are also practiced.

Most consequential, Les employs behavioral role-play with students. This way, students understand, "What is being asked of them and why?" For instance, Les role-plays a scenario when the teacher poses a question to a student, requiring wait time. While the student asked searches for the answer, Les encourages other students to raise their hands, and even make noise to gain his attention. When Les circles back and asks the student who was picked how the other students' actions made him or her feel, words like "frustration" quickly appeared. For the second role-play setup, Les again asks the same student another difficult question. However, Les had the class sit quietly. In fact, after a few moments, Les solicited encouragement like "You can do it, Doug" from his other students. This time, the student felt supported.

By practicing behaviors, Les has created a classroom environment that is both nurturing and productive.

4. _It's Not a "Set-It-and-Forget-It" Approach_: Educators must embrace and embody the concept of a lifelong learner. Through

articles, discussions, workshops, and courses, there is always a way to improve, hone, and refresh skills. As Les reflects, many of the skills he utilizes today were not taught in his undergraduate studies. Technology-related skills, such as desktop publishing and non-linear video editing, were learned well after his formal education. Les believes, "Good educators must have an unquenchable thirst for knowledge." This intellectual curiosity needs to exist so that the status quo can be viewed with a critical eye.

As an example, Les suggests reevaluating how school facilities are operated. While schools are regularly open during the academic year at daytime, he recommends not having them closed in the evenings and summers. School facilities are a powerful place for learning and activity. They should be made available so that the public can use the computers, gym, pool, and classrooms. This would attract a cross-generational section of the local population, creating stronger community. In the end, it would truly represent the best and highest use of taxpayer facilities and monies.

5. _Show Students How to Solve Problems, But Don't Solve Problems for Them_: As teachers, it is often difficult to see students struggle and make mistakes. At the same time, Les believes, "A mistake can be a great teaching vehicle, if a student learns and grows from it." Les has tremendous confidence in students' ability to solve problems. Teachers may provide a construct to assist students, but the problem-solving belongs to the pupils in the classroom. This philosophy is intrinsic to his teaching. If students are given the opportunity "to critically evaluate their work and use what they find to keep improving," then growth and development ensue. Les quotes Randy Pausch who wrote, "In the end, educators best serve students by helping

them be more self-reflective." For Les, learning is not always linear. It requires introspection. Sometimes, you have to stop and reflect.

**Other Interview Questions**
*1. Who is/are your role model(s) from an educational perspective?*

Without any hesitation, Les states that his father, a former teacher and principal, is his role model. What set his father apart is that he understood young people, was an advocate, and knew how to relate to kids. Les shared that his father always "did right" by the students, and for that, he was loved.

Sadly, Les' father passed away at the early age of 48. Perhaps one of the best commemorations to his life is that his funeral procession stretched greater than a mile and the number of hours for viewing had to be doubled. Les states, "That is a life of impact and significance."

*2. When you take a look at teachers, in general, and recognize all the hard work and devotion they put into their jobs, what would you say is the one thing that you think teachers can improve upon so they can become more highly effective?*

Les believes that teachers are notoriously humble. It is an occupation that serves the greater good and makes certain the next generation succeeds. Teachers deflect praise and the limelight so frequently that many believe that they have nothing to do with student successes. Les feels that teachers should learn to take some credit. After all, teachers have everything to do with grooming and nurturing young people for the world that awaits them.

*3. Are there policies that your school (or past school) has adopted which allow teachers to excel?*

The issue of human capital remains one of the most important aspects of schools. Finding and hiring the best and brightest educators and administrators are the keys for success. No matter how benign or unhelpful school policies may be or appear, exceptional teachers will always find a way to excel.

*4. In order to improve our educational system, what are the shortcomings you notice in schools. What are some of the good things happening? What do you think needs to change?*

One of the most significant shortcomings is what Les calls, "Sending the wrong message." This exists on a variety of levels from promoting specific programs, like athletics over academics, to failing to practice what is preached (e.g., teaching civics and stressing the value of democracy, but running the school in a way that is anything but democratic). Les shares, "Students pick up on this almost subliminal message." They can infer what is important in the eyes of society and can figure out the contradictory messages.

As an example, Les shares how the local community enthusiastically supports scholastic athletic competitions. Yet, the same passion is not shown to academic accomplishments like science fairs. This is further exacerbated by what the local media chooses to cover such as sports and sensation stories. Les states, "Teachers, as well as school districts, send these [wrong] messages and good educators must be aware of the messages they are sending."

Lastly, Les believes in eliminating dress codes, specifically regarding appropriate colors. Les opines, "[Dress codes say] We're more concerned about what you look like than the content of your character." While dress codes are deemed to cut down on disciplinary issues, Les has observed the complete opposite. He states, "Educators should provide opportunities for students to express themselves in appropriate ways. [But] Attempting to limit the way students express themselves is like squeezing a balloon. You can control one area, but lose control somewhere else."

# CHAPTER 13

## Burt Saxon

Connecticut State Teacher of the Year (2005)
(U.S. History, Psychology – Grades 10 to 12)

*"A successful teaching career is a marathon, not a sprint."*

— *Anonymous*

As a veteran educator of over 35 years, Burt Saxon's secret of longevity in teaching is building expertise in multiple subjects and enhancing skills over the course of a career. Burt knows that it is vital for teachers to "not burn themselves into the ground the first couple of years." Otherwise, departure from the teaching industry is inevitable, explaining why so many good teachers leave the teaching profession.

When Burt first heard the quote above, he shares, "It really sank in. That really made sense to me." In his own experience, Burt charged so hard at the beginning of his teaching career that he felt exhausted after only five years. He reflects, "I taught for five years and was so tired." To rejuvenate as well as augment his skills, Burt pursued and completed doctoral studies at Teachers College, Columbia University. Thereafter, Burt returned to the classroom, but this time he was armed with greater experience and know-how. "When I came back from my doctorate, I was a lot smarter and didn't burn myself out. [In fact] I stayed another 28 years," says Burt.

So what's Burt's advice? He answers, "Take each year at a time, each week at a time, each day at a time, and each class at a time. Enjoy the journey." He adds, "I enjoyed teaching classes, tried to stay out of political issues…my job was to teach kids and that's what I tried to do."

## Background

Burt Saxon is a rock star among his inner city students. On any given day, students call his name in the hallway and seek to hug him. He is definitely a student's kind of teacher. However, that was not always the case. Burt's formative years were strictly small town and mid-western in rural Plainfield, Illinois. He attended a public school, participated in sports, and played in the band. As a college student, Burt's goal was to become a teacher in an urban education setting, even though he knew that many urban schools exist in high poverty areas. Burt declares, "My goal then was to become a high school social studies teacher, perhaps in an inner city high school.…But the question that troubled me was whether I had what it took as a person to succeed in an inner city school [based on his own ethnicity]."

Through compassion for his students and an ability to make learning easy and fun, Burt's successes answer his earlier query with a definitive, "Yes!" Burt's former students rave about his influence in their lives. Many have been inspired to become teachers, while others have entered law and medicine. The fact is obvious that Burt's teaching philosophy – be a mentor, a friend, and get to know your students outside of the classroom – works. That is why many students see Burt as a second parent. In fact, it is not unusual for Burt to coach students who are studying for the SATs, take students on college visits, write dozens of letters of recommendations, and attend all sorts of student athletic games, even when it rains. Burt states, "I think all educators, whatever type of kids you're teaching, want to be on the lookout for the kids at risk. And you want to try and do whatever you can…maybe a little mentoring. I think that's a fundamental part of the profession."

For over 30 years, Burt taught at the high school level. He has also remained active in post-secondary education, teaching at Yale University and Southern Connecticut State University. Burt's many accomplishments include five-time Yale-New Haven Teachers Institute Fellow as well as the 2005 Connecticut State Teacher of the Year and New Haven Teacher of the Year. Quinnipiac University also granted Burt an honorary doctorate. In addition to teaching, Burt has co-authored numerous books in psychology, history, and economics.

Burt received his bachelor's degree in economics at Carleton College and master's degree in teaching at Wesleyan University. He also holds a doctorate of education from Teachers College, Columbia University.

**Teacher Top 5**

1. _Make a Lifelong Commitment to Becoming a Better Teacher_: All too often after years of teaching, routine can set in and the status quo can be quite comfortable. Burt encourages educators to better themselves each year. He says, "Try to do a little something every year to improve your skills." This can take many forms, but meaningful professional development that is subject-based and usually takes at least a week are the best. Burt states, "Much of [in-service training] isn't great…and one shot, two-hour sessions are rarely helpful. Summer institutes that go for one week can be very good."

The key, though, is finding professional development opportunities that not only resonate with a teacher's interest, but is also something that can improve his or her skills. Burt differentiates between subject-matter and instructional training. In his experience, all of the worthwhile continuing education has been to improve subject skills. Burt comments, "Having professional development with people who know a lot more about a subject than I do is very, very helpful." Instructional training, on the other hand, can be lackluster. Burt believes that most teachers figure out a teaching style that works for them. Hence, professional development should be targeted to enhance subject skills. Some of Burt's most rewarding professional development experiences include his work at the Yale School of Medicine, where they helped develop skills to teach human sexuality; University of Massachusetts in International Relations, where he learned about languages and world culture for a magnate program; and Trinity College, where he studied African American literature.

2. _Love Both the Subject-Matter and the Age Group Taught_: To be a successful and happy teacher, it is enormously important to enjoy

not only the subject-matter taught, but also the age group of the students. Burt states, "Some like middle school, some like elementary school…if you like the subject and age group, you're getting paid to do something you like. How can you beat that?" While it is often believed that high school teachers are more interested in the subject rather than teenage adolescence, and elementary school teachers like young children more so than the subjects taught, Burt does not think these characteristics should be mutually exclusive. In order to find happiness in teaching, Burt recommends, "Create a situation where you can enjoy the age group and subject." That is one of the secrets for longevity in the classroom.

3. *Mentoring Is At Least As Important As Teaching*: Mentoring exists in all different forms. It can simply be spending time and talking with students. It can be reaching out to form a mentor-mentee relationship where guidance is needed. Either way, mentoring broadens a teacher's impact beyond instruction. In speaking about mentoring, Burt says, "That is where the real impact is. You can't mentor 125 kids, but you can mentor a few each year. They seek you out and you seek them out."

Among his many student-teacher stories, Burt shares one about a young person who always came to school an hour before school. While Burt prepped for class, they would talk every morning, eventually developing a solid rapport. Burt knew about the student's challenging family background, how he aspired to be a professional football coach, and what he was doing to accomplish his dreams. Each day, they would talk. Burt knew that he was playing the role of a caring adult and teacher, who could lend a sympathetic ear. Fast-forward many years later, and this student became a college football coach, and ultimately, a coach in the National Football League. Mentoring is about getting to know and help others beyond the responsibilities delineated in a job description.

Mentoring also takes the shape of guiding other teachers and colleagues. Student teachers are a good example, especially when master teachers have a wealth of knowledge to share. Reflecting on the numerous student teachers he has mentored, Burt says, "What I'm proud of is that they're still teachers!"

4. _Teach in an Authoritative Way, Not a Repressive (Authoritarian) or Permissive Way_: Based on Diana Baumrind's research on parenting styles, Burt applies this same framework to teaching styles. He asserts, "I am a strong believer of authoritative teaching, especially in the inner city." Authoritative teaching is typically defined as establishing rules and guidelines in order to provide structure in the classroom. Nurturing and assertiveness are a big part of it, and forgiveness and support are essential. Burt declares, "If you use authoritative teaching, make some demands on kids, but provide incredible support. Support is critical!" In this case, support means showing interest, care, and compassion. Burt attends after-school games and events. He also gives his home telephone number to vulnerable students, just in case they have problems over the weekend. He carves out time to speak with students before and after school. He even avails himself in his classroom to students during lunch.

In executing authoritative teaching, Burt cautions, "Never do anything physical. Never humiliate a child. Never speak to the child in a harsh tone in front of a peer group. Do it privately. I guarantee it works, because I saw it work and I used it." To address his critics,

Burt states, "It doesn't build resentment. Instead, it builds a strong student-teacher relationship."

5. _Run a Highly Organized Classroom (Even If It Does Not Appear So)_: While it may appear obvious, strong organization is vital so that a class can be run efficiently and effectively. Burt says, "Know where everything is…books, band-aids, scissors…make enough copies…you don't want to run to the copy machine in the middle of class." Instructional time is limited enough. Therefore, prepping materials and lessons beforehand allow class to run on time. Burt remembers incidents where parents were upset at some of Burt's fellow colleagues because they were unable to start class punctually. He recalls a parent stating that she walked into her child's class and observed that 19 minutes passed before instruction even began. Burt confesses, "I can understand how parents can be unhappy if there is disorganization in a class." In his own teaching, Burt tries to start class within one minute. He shares, "It is a skill to have in high school that you have to work on."

**Other Interview Questions**

_1. Who is/are your role model(s) from an educational perspective?_

There have been several role models in Burt's life. Without a doubt, Juanita Niehus, his high school Latin teacher, was the most impactful. Burt says, "Mrs. Niehus was by far his best teacher. She was superior and I wouldn't doubt it if she was the best Latin teacher in the whole country." When asked what made Mrs. Niehus so special, Burt shares, "First, she knew Latin inside-out. Second, Mrs. Niehus would take students to the National Convention (National Junior Classical League) during the summer." Burt and his fellow students would travel on a bus – picking up students all across the country – to a variety of universities to compete. At times, there would be up to 60 students. Burt comments, "Mrs. Niehus was the only chaperone and nobody ever misbehaved." In one competition, Burt fared well. The experience opened his eyes. It gave Burt the confidence that he would do fine, if he decided to attend an academically rigorous college. For that, Burt confesses, "I was always grateful to Mrs. Niehus."

Burt also identifies his economics professor from Carleton College, Ada Mae Harrison, as one of his role models. From Teachers College, Columbia University, Burt acknowledges Lawrence Cremin, his history of education professor. "Both were great scholars and teachers," says Burt. He applauds their strong depth of knowledge, ability to question and avoid dogmatism, and openness to multiple perspectives.

In terms of educational researchers, Burt has great respect for James Comer, a notable child psychiatrist at Yale; Diane Ravitch, a professor and historian of education at New York University; and Linda Darling-Hammond, a professor and author at Stanford University.

*2. When you take a look at teachers, in general, and recognize all the hard work and devotion they put into their jobs, what would you say is the one thing that you think teachers can improve upon so they can become more highly effective?*

Many teachers have the impression that working hard is more important than working efficiently. Burt says, "It's the other way around." The reality of teaching is that teachers must find ways to work efficiently so that the workload is manageable. When his class is watching a movie and students are executing a self-directed question sheet, Burt is often grading papers at the back of the room. While some teachers may frown on this, Burt disagrees. At the back of the room, he can multi-task by monitoring his class and catching up on his work. In regards to grading, he comments, "I'm not going to have to grade papers until 2AM, because I've done some work at school… otherwise, the job would be impossible."

*3. Are there policies that your school (or past school) has adopted which allow teachers to excel?*

When it comes to policies, Burt believes that the most important thing for a teacher is to find an exceptional and supportive administrator with whom he or she feels comfortable. Burt states, "You need to work for people who respect teachers and who want teachers to excel." The last thing a teacher wants is an administrator who is ineffective, or worse, undermines teachers. In his 42 years of experience at the high school and college level, Burt has encountered the good and the bad. At a community college where he taught, Burt had high praise for his administrator. Burt says, "She was sensational. She was very oriented towards kids, efficient, and organized." Over his teaching career, Burt has worked with some incredible administrators who deserve recognition, including Lonnie Garris Jr. at Hillhouse High School, Wendy Samberg at Gateway Community College, and Cheryl Durwin at Southern Connecticut State University.

*4. In order to improve our educational system, what are the shortcomings you notice in schools. What are some of the good things happening? What do you think needs to change?*

From Burt's perspective, education needs to be much more teacher-centric and less administrator-focused. Burt declares, "Teaching needs to become more important than administering. It always has been more important, but no one wants to admit it." Teaching is the core of the profession, but the number of classroom teachers has declined over time. Layers of additional professionals, such as literacy coaches, have padded the system. If Burt could have it his way, he would streamline administration. When additional monies exist, Burt would hire more teachers as opposed to adding layers. Burt also makes a point to say that teachers need to be held to high standards. While tenure is part of the educational system, all teachers should be held accountable. Burt states, "Let's do something so good teachers are supported and rewarded, and people who don't belong in the profession can see it quickly and get out."

# CHAPTER 14

**Pamela Harman**
Alabama State Teacher of the Year (2008)
(Earth Science – Grades 11 to 12)

*"If I have seen further than others, it is by standing upon the shoulders of giants."*
— *Sir Isaac Newton*

Pamela Harman is not only a first-rate teacher, but also extraordinarily humble and gracious. She credits her vast accomplishments to all of the individuals who have helped her achieve and grow as an educator. That is why she loves Newton's quote. Pamela states, "Becoming a great teacher is surrounding yourself with people who are better than you."

For Pamela, this began at the University of Alabama at Birmingham. In her undergraduate program, she was heavily influenced by Dr. Lee Meadows, one of the leading experts on inquiry science instruction at the secondary level. Pamela points out that Dr. Meadows helped her understand inquiry learning at the highest level. She declares, "His classes helped me learn content mapping and how to connect with students."

Later, Pamela met Tammy Dunn, the 2003 Alabama State Teacher of the Year. Pamela taught at the same school as Mrs. Dunn who served as the science department head. "[Tammy] had high expectations of teachers. Don't sit on your laurels. Teachers need to grow and get better," recounts Pamela. Through Mrs. Dunn's leadership, Pamela believes that she became a better teacher. She observed Mrs. Dunn on numerous occasions, watching how she taught and how she connected with students.

Then, there was Marla Hines, an applied physical science teacher, who was selected as the alternate Alabama Teacher of the Year for 2011. Pamela had the opportunity to team up with Mrs. Hines and it was wonderful. "It gave me a colleague to collaborate with, to talk to. What did inquiry instruction in the classroom look like? How do you make it work most effectively?" says Pamela.

Pamela sincerely appreciates and understands the value of surrounding herself with outstanding teachers – to listen, observe, and learn. That is what has allowed her to achieve a level of excellence in her own teaching.

## Background

Pamela Harman is a remarkable role model and a tremendous example of what can be accomplished through perseverance and hard work. Even though Pamela always knew that she would be an educator, her path to teaching was not easy.

During her formative years, Pamela faced family challenges and economic hardships. At 12 years of age, her father left, creating a paternal void and financial strain. Pamela and her brother were raised by a single mother who worked at the local fabric supply company. For as long as she can remember, Pamela also worked to help support her family, taking on various jobs. Upon high school graduation, Pamela received a scholarship to attend college. There, she flourished. However, life has a way of throwing in twists and turns. In college, Pamela's mother passed away. To exacerbate the situation, her scholarship ran out, adding to her economic hardship. Facing overwhelming adversity, Pamela left school, decided to enlist in the United States Marine Corps, and carried on. When she was not in field training or deployed, such as serving in the Gulf War, Pamela took classes.

About a decade after her military service, Pamela graduated from the University of Alabama at Birmingham, becoming the first in her family to receive a college degree. She also earned her master's of science degree from Mississippi State University. As a lifelong learner, she is now studying at Walden University to obtain her doctorate in teacher leadership.

All of these experiences have helped shape Pamela and make her passionate about providing an education for those who struggle for such opportunities. She states, "Everyday you make choices. You can't let those things happening in your life dictate who you are going to be in the future and take away opportunities....You can't let life's circumstances steal that away from you."

Pamela is a National Board Certified Teacher and was recognized as Alabama's 2008 State Teacher of the Year.

## Teacher Top 5

1. _Promote High Expectations_: On the first day of school, Pamela always communicates to her students that they are going to be challenged to ask questions and figure things out. "Learning is about being pushed beyond your regular abilities," asserts Pamela. She continues, "You must believe that all students deserve to be pushed to their highest level of achievable mastery. Every student deserves a chance toward future success. High expectations provide the doorway." Oftentimes, when a teacher has high expectations of his or her students, they will not only meet their full potential, but also exceed them.

In order to guide students to the next level, Pamela pre-assesses throughout the year to determine what her students know. Formal assessments also follow. For Pamela, her favorite thing to hear from students is, "Mrs. Harman, I learned something new today." She explains, "That is how it should be in every classroom."

2. _Develop Strong Content Mastery_: According to Pamela, good teachers are good connectors. They take the existing knowledge that students possess, help them connect it to the current content being studied, and build the foundation for what they will need in

the future. How do you accomplish that? It is strong content mastery. How do you secure content mastery? Pamela suggests a "never stop learning" attitude. Educators can earn a degree in their chosen content area or read professional journals. Either way, it is imperative that teachers are knowledgeable and stay up-to-date. Pamela insists, "With content mastery, you can make learning authentic and fully accessible to students." She continues, "Content mastery gives you confidence and allows you to make important connections to the content for students."

3. _Know Your Students_: "Every student deserves to have a teacher who knows him or her as a person and cares about his or her personal and educational well-being. When students know that the teacher sees them as individuals, they will go to extraordinary lengths to be successful in that class," shares Pamela. This relationship building is a key ingredient to her success.

On the first day of school, Pamela implements an "Ice Breaker/Get to Know Your Teacher and Peers" activity. She passes out index cards and asks students to write their first name and last initial. Thereafter, students must write or draw what they like and what is important to them. Each student card is then disclosed to the class, building camaraderie and creating a community of learners. Pamela also participates, sharing even intimate facts like the year when her own brother committed suicide. To her students, she reveals, "I lost someone significant in my life...I'll give you all that I've got, but some days [at school] will be very hard for me." This candor and sharing are important so that a student-teacher connection is formed. Separately, Pamela also takes inventory of student personalities and learning modalities. That way, she knows who each student is as a person and learner, allowing her to tailor instruction to each individual's needs.

Building rapport takes time, but at the end of the day, Pamela quotes Carl Buehner who stated, "They [students] may forget what you said, but they will never forget how you made them feel."

4. *Possess Enthusiasm and Passion for What You Teach*: No matter what grade level taught, teachers must have enthusiasm and passion. Pamela believes, "You owe it to your students to be 'on' and have full energy every day. Kids deserve to get the best out of me and to see my passion and what I love to do." In fact, she calls this the "Secret Weapon" of teaching. That's because Pamela knows, "if you are excited and passionate about the content, students can't help but be interested too." It also goes the other way. If the teacher does not love what is being taught, then how can students be convinced it is worthwhile to know? As an earth science teacher, Pamela teaches about rocks, which is not always the most exciting topic. That said, if the lesson is created and delivered so that it is engaging, stimulating, and student-centered, students will love to learn and want to show up to the classroom.

5. *Engage in Reflective Practice*: As a lifelong learner, Pamela embraces self-reflection to improve as a teacher. She does so formally – taking meticulous notes for each lesson – and informally – thinking deeply about what worked. Pamela states, "I am constantly looking at my teaching practices and trying to improve. I listen and watch other educators to find best teaching practices that I can also use in my class." In science education, Pamela is always trying new things. Therefore, it is important to be honest when self-evaluating one's

own work. Sometimes, the issue might be sequencing to figure out what aspect of the lesson should have gone first or otherwise. Other times, it might be timing to allow for comprehension and questions. No matter how large or small the issue, Pamela's goal is to learn and grow as an educator. So long as a willingness to improve exists, self-reflection is a great technique to hone a teacher's craft.

## Other Interview Questions
*1. Who is/are your role model(s) from an educational perspective?*

As the head of Pamela's science department, Tammy Dunn, the 2003 Alabama State Teacher of the Year, left an indelible impression. Pamela acknowledges, "Tammy Dunn...is the person that shaped who I am as a teacher. She set high standards for personal excellence that I have always tried to live up to. Her philosophy of teaching always centered on student learning. She ingrained in me that teaching is not about me, it is everyday about students and student learning....I owe a lot of who I am as a teacher to her." Pamela adds that it is important for teachers to find a role model. That cannot be done in isolation by closing the door to his or her classroom. She suggests seeking out other teachers who are doing good work or reading academic journals that focus on best practices.

*2. When you take a look at teachers, in general, and recognize all the hard work and devotion they put into their jobs, what would you say is the one thing that you think teachers can improve upon so they can become more highly effective?*

Throughout an educator's career, it is imperative to seek out best practices proactively and learn from others. Pamela encourages, "Open your door to other educators and go see what others are doing in their classrooms…if I am not looking at the practices of others, then I am using myself as a measuring stick. I could be terrible and just not know it, because I have never seen the better practices that are out there." Moreover, there is nothing wrong about taking something that someone has already implemented, especially when it works. Pamela suggests modifying what ideas you find compelling to your own content, instruction, and style. After all, imitation truly is the greatest form of flattery.

*3. Are there policies that your school (or past school) has adopted which allow teachers to excel?*

In order to improve the teaching profession, a quality mentoring program for new teachers is essential. Master teachers can impart knowledge, model teaching, and help guide, as well as act as a confidante. Pamela posits, "Strong collegial relationships deter isolation and promote an atmosphere of oneness among teachers." She also points out that seasoned teachers can learn from new teachers. Fresh ideas and a different way of looking at things are always welcome. Lastly, mentor programs should not be authoritarian. Rather, they should be based on a foundation of collaboration and learning.

*4. In order to improve our educational system, what are the shortcomings you notice in schools? What are some of the good things happening? What do you think needs to change?*

In a global and competitive economy, real-world skills and applications are a must. Pamela identifies, "We need to be instilling 21st century skills, like written and oral communication, collaboration, critical thinking, and global perspectives into the classroom." When students graduate and finally attain a job, they need to be problem solvers, and comfortable with asking questions and stating their opinions. "I don't want students to leave my classroom and not be critical thinkers....Our students are going to be competing for jobs, not with the person sitting next to them, but with students in India, China, and Japan. We need to be preparing them to be competitive," says Pamela.

Using technology to enhance learning and empower students toward understanding is a good thing. "Technology cannot be used just for the sake of using it," notes Pamela. "Instead, I see many teachers making the use of technology as a part of an effective component of teaching the content." In one of Pamela's science activities, students learn about a historical scientist and design a lesson. They then share what they learned with students in another school. Students utilized the Internet to perform research and employed Skype to deliver the lesson. The collaborating school used websites like Poll Everywhere to pre-assess, Wallwisher to post ideas, and Museum Box to build stories. All of these technology tools are student-centered and elevate the learning experience.

# CHAPTER 15

## Ronald Poplau
National Teachers Hall of Fame Inductee (1999)
(Community Service – Grades 11 to 12)

*"The Doer of Good Becomes Good."*

— *Shawnee Mission Northwest High School (1992 Community Commitment Class)*

Ronald Poplau's inaugural community service class began in 1992. Back then, it was a brand new experiment in the high school curriculum with 17 students enrolled. The following semester, Ron's class was so heavily oversubscribed that he had to turn away dozens of students. To accommodate the demand, Ron taught six classes. Even then, students were still clamoring to get into his class. Ron states,

"At one time, we had almost half the school enrolled in community service."

For its popularity, the true measure of community services' success is the ability to create transformative, life-changing perspective for any person who serves. Explaining the quote above, Ron paraphrases child psychologist and writer, Bruno Bettelheim, declaring, "It is possible for us to lose our humanity. We have to continually work at it." That is why Ron says, "We are what we do…[and] we have to work at being good." All too often, Ron hears adults saying to kids, "Do as I say, and don't do as I do." The truth to the matter is that children are going to do what we do, and not what we say. The modeling of good deeds and actions is imperative to develop young people who are caring and altruistic. For that reason and many more, community service is essential and imparts to the participant a good sense of self in becoming a compassionate and productive citizen.

## Background

"Giving back" is an often hackneyed expression based on varying degrees of commitment. For Ron Poplau, he's all in, all of the time. Ron's path to education was inspired by his father's journey to America from Germany at the turn of the century. As a new immigrant, Ron's dad never received a formal education due to prejudice and fear. He remained illiterate throughout his entire life and relied on his family to assist with reading and writing. Things many of us take for granted, such as reading road signs and writing letters, required the help of others. His father's circumstances deeply affected Ron. In one generation, Ron turned it around. In fact, Ron's decision to become an educator and give others the power of learning and life skills, that was deprived of his father, shines light on what individuals can accomplish.

In a teaching career that spans over 50 years, Ron first began as a social studies teacher in 1962. Over time, he incorporated volunteer-based projects in his curriculum. Due to its popularity, Ron founded a community service elective known as Cougars Community Commitment in 1992. Since then, Ron and his students have helped thousands of low-income, disadvantaged, disabled people, and seniors through educational tutoring, food drives and deliveries, fundraisers, visits to retirement homes, and so forth. Ron's legacy of giving back to the community and developing young people to care more than simply about themselves compelled him to write *Doer of Good Becomes Good*, a tell-all book about how community service positively affects schools.

For his many accomplishments, Ron has been recognized by numerous organizations and institutions. He is an inductee to the National Teachers Hall of Fame, Mid-America Education Hall of Fame, and Kansas Teachers Hall of Fame. He was named 2006 Kansas State Teacher of the Year and National Teacher of the Year finalist. Ron was also awarded as a Disney Hands Teacher and Shawnee Citizen of the Year. The United States State Department also asked Ron to serve as a teacher-diplomat to Russia, sharing his know-how about community service.

Ron received his bachelor's degree at St. Thomas College and master's at Emporia State University.

**Teacher Top 5**

1. *Establish a Student Advisory Board for Every Class*: Allowing students to give input is vitally important. It provides student ownership and a real sense of responsibility. The old adage, "People support a world they help create," absolutely applies. Ron's student advisory board consists of a president, vice president, and five students. Every Thursday, they meet for 95 minutes to talk about possible projects for the class. Ron states, "I learned that in my first year of teaching back in 1962…[to] have a student advisory board for every class…. When students have an input and you listen to them, they'll come through every single time." In this student-centric model, the teacher guides students via inductive teaching while also helping teach critical thinking skills. It communicates to students that it is a shared learning experience and that their voice matters.

2. *Provide a Great Deal of Community Service or Service Learning Opportunities*: If there is a will, there is a way, especially when it comes to service. After all, Ron states, "Virtue is its own reward." One of Ron's most impressive student-driven projects includes bringing media attention to a young boy who was suffering from a genetic birth deformity called spondylothoracic dysplasia. The condition leads to a severe lack of growth in the spine and the rib cage. As a result, space is limited for the organs in this area, particularly the lungs, to develop and grow. Almost always, the prognosis is lethal without surgery. While health insurance denied the young boy's claim, Ron's students approached the local television station to promote the desperate plight of this boy. After a week of televised attention and tremendous community outcry, the insurance company acquiesced and paid for the surgery. Student activism was

essential in saving this young boy's life. Other meaningful projects include organizing a bone marrow transplant match, raising money for Smile Train to remedy cleft lip, and partnering with inner city schools. No matter what the cause, all students, with the guidance and encouragement of their teachers, should dream as large as they can in coming up with ideas.

3. _Develop a Trust With Your Students_: The author, Barbara Smith, said, "Trust is to human relationships what faith is to gospel living. It is the beginning place, the foundation upon which more can be built. Where trust is, love can flourish." This holds true with student-teacher relationships. In the first week of class, Ron lets students know that it is their classroom and they have a voice. He shares the school's community service legacy, setting the stage of high expectations. Soon after, Ron establishes a student advisory board. From there, the potential for growth and learning is limitless. Ron states, "Given the opportunity, kids will always rise to the level of your expectations…. It's absolutely amazing how many students are so highly motivated that some clock in more than 1,000 hours of service."

4. _Don't Be Afraid to Take Risks_: Risk-taking can mean different things to different people. For a community service teacher, Ron says, "A risk to me simply means what you are doing could possibly cost you your job." In that case, no matter what the risk, students must understand the purpose of any project. Over his career, Ron has taken on numerous risks to expose students to multiple perspectives of race relations, including hate groups like the Ku Klux Klan and Black Muslims. He has also brought in controversial speakers such as Pete O'Neal, the former chairman of the Kansas City chapter of the Black Panther Party, and Henry Floyd Brown, the last man

on death row in Kansas State Prison. Perhaps the most precarious venture was a school field trip an inner city housing project which, unfortunately, ended in their forced detention and robbery. That said, Ron does not believe adversity should deter good intentions. He points out, "I think if you take a risk, and the kids know you're taking a risk for their benefit, they'll support you."

5. _Become Involved in Your Community_: There is no replacement for first-hand experience, especially when it comes to community service. Ron highly encourages teachers and students to get involved with their community. For teachers, in particular, Ron declares, "It adds a certain amount of validity, because you'll teach from your strengths and experience. If the only thing you have is book knowledge…kids will tune you out." As a case in point, Ron's past experience having worked 11 years at the Kansas State Prison was enormously helpful in their unit of study on crime. Combining guest speakers and Ron's own perspective, students were treated to oral records that were real and riveting. "Real-life examples help a great deal," says Ron.

**Other Interview Questions**

_1. Who is/are your role model(s) from an educational perspective?_

Woodrow Wilson was an academic, teacher, and the 28th President of the United States. Ron states, "He was the best President as far as I'm concerned. He's everything that I would want to be as a teacher and person." Prior to becoming President, Wilson taught at Bryn Mawr, Wesleyan University, and Princeton. He eventually became president of Princeton University. As part of the Princeton curriculum, Wilson advocated for the inclusion of community service. Ron adds, "I am a great admirer of Woodrow Wilson. I agree with his concept of education: make it a preparation for life and stress community service."

*2. When you take a look at teachers, in general, and recognize all the hard work and devotion they put into their jobs, what would you say is the one thing that you think teachers can improve upon so they can become more highly effective?*

Isolation is one of the worst things that can happen to a teacher. This can exist singularly or as a group – all teachers in the same subject-matter. Ron asserts, "Don't isolate yourself. Develop a team approach and feed off of other's strong points." Ron believes that all sciences and language arts should be housed together, because there is a lot of cross-curriculum material. Ron continues, "Teachers need to get a whole perspective of what's being done rather than what we're doing."

In terms of community service, Ron shares, "Every teacher should espouse a cause that means something to their students. It leads to credibility." This is especially true when real-life experiences can be brought back into the classroom. Another mode of creating authentic experiences is to seek out guest speakers. Ron comments, "Tap into their expertise. I averaged 70 guest speakers per semester. Kids loved it."

*3. Are there policies that your school (or past school) has adopted which allow teachers to excel?*

Having a supportive principal who trusts and provides latitude to teachers is one of the most outstanding qualities a school can possess. Ron says, "Our principal is a strong backer of teachers and he encourages us to do our best....He is one of the finest principals for whom I have ever worked." Ron deems that the ideal principal is one who is an educational leader. This type of administrator takes the time to get to know his or her faculty and spends time in the classrooms. Praise and recognition are given easily when deserved, but constructive criticism and consequences also exist when necessary. Ron points out that when a parent calls to complain, his principal handles it, allowing teachers to focus on what they do best: teach.

*4. In order to improve our educational system, what are the shortcomings you notice in schools. What are some of the good things happening? What do you think needs to change?*

Quite succinctly, Ron declares, "Get rid of No Child Left Behind." He believes that education should not be reduced to passing an exam. The reality, unfortunately, is that teachers will teach to the test. This defeats the purpose of learning, in Ron's opinion, especially when students will forget what was taught after the test is over. To circumvent some of the issues existing in schools, Ron suggest giving students choice. Students should be given the opportunity to choose their teachers. Ron analogizes, "If you like the doctor you go to, you tell other people. If you don't like the doctor, you go somewhere else. The same goes with lawyers." This is what should happen with teachers. Even if students do not get their first choice, Ron says, "At least they had an option, a chance….Education isn't indoctrination, not the filling up of the mind. It's a pulling out of the student what's inside. We have got to get kids to want to learn."

# CHAPTER 16

## Robert Feurer
Nebraska State Teacher of the Year (2011)
(Science – Grades 7 to 12)

*"Education is not the filling of a pail, but the lighting of a fire."*
— *William Butler Yeats*

While some argue about who originated the above quote, no one can debate the incredible responsibility of the educator to do more than just teach curriculum. After all, the ultimate goal is to instill in students the love of learning. Bob Feurer sees Yeats' quote as a great metaphor about education. Bob states, "Education is a fire. You light it. Feed it. It grows. It gets bigger. It's an awesome definition of how we all should be as learners."

All too often, education can appear somewhat limited. Bob gives the example of a questionnaire where there are ten blanks. Some students fill in the ten blanks and think their education is completely done. "Education is often the same way. It's defined and has defined limits. That can't be the case, because [education should be a] fire that continues to spread," says Bob.

As a teacher, Bob is a lifelong learner who knows that his job is never done, and he continues to grow all the time. That is what he tries to instill in his students. Life's answers are not a timed, multiple choice assessment. Rather, it's about discovery, figuring things out, and taking pleasure in the inquiry. Bob says, "I teach to give my students seeing eyes, not just sight."

## Background

Bob never intended to be a teacher. In fact, he resisted. It was his mother, a former teacher, who is responsible for showing him what teaching can do for others. It was a good thing, because Bob became an exceptional educator. From wrestling coach to science teacher, Bob's passion for learning is palpable and his ability to develop relationships with students, inside and outside of the classroom, is one of the secrets to his success. "I'm a teacher who loves what he does every day, and I love all my kids," says Bob.

Even after more than 35 years of teaching, Bob still considers himself an artisan teacher. He utilizes textbooks more as references as opposed to guiding instruction. He takes pleasure in creating original content, making lessons relevant and easy to comprehend. One former student shares, "He makes you get what he's teaching. He'll keep finding things symbolizing what he's teaching and make you get it." Perhaps that is because Bob's teaching style is genuinely authentic in learning. Bob says, "I try to make my students scientists, not teach them science. I do not want my students to study biology. I want them to become biologists."

At his school, Bob is famous for acting as curator to the 22-acre arboretum which he calls an outdoor classroom. With past and current students, he has worked tirelessly, planting over 1,200 trees and digging a 1,700 gallon pond that houses goldfish. The arboretum is the classroom for the myriad of science courses taught, including biology, global science, and anatomy/physiology.

Apart from teaching science, Bob is very active in after-school activities, having coached a variety of sports like wrestling, football, and track and field. For the larger community, Bob serves as adjunct faculty to a number of colleges in Nebraska such as Peru State College and Metropolitan Community College.

Over his career, Bob has been recognized and awarded honors by numerous organizations. In 2011, Bob was named Nebraska State Teacher of the Year. He was also the Nebraska Presidential Awardee for Excellence in Math and Science Teaching. Bob also served as President of Nebraska Scholastic Wrestling Coaches Association and President of Nebraska Association of Teachers of Science.

Bob earned his bachelor's degree in biological and physical science, and master's degree in math and science teaching at the University of Nebraska at Kearney.

**Teacher Top 5**

1. *Get to Know Your Students Well*: When teachers know their students really well, they can cater to their strengths, make personal connections, and help them meet and exceed their full potential. For Bob, having longevity teaching at the same school helps. He has taught at his school in Nebraska for over 35 years. At this point, he is teaching the children of former students and the entire community knows him. Just as importantly, Bob teaches seventh graders as well as eleventh and twelfth graders. This is a huge advantage as compared to other teachers who may have moved around or teach only one grade. Bob states, "You get to know the students' backgrounds, likes and dislikes, strengths and weaknesses…kids also get to know me. Those who had me in seventh…know my expectations."

To become acquainted with students, Bob always starts with a survey early on in the year. He asks about siblings, full names, extended family relationships, and such. Bob also taps into the school data system to find the first person of contact, in order to understand a student's home life, without having to pry publicly. Bob knows, "Kids have a difficult time disassociating home life with school life. Usually, if they have a problem in school, there's an issue at home." Bob also builds rapport outside of the classroom. His friendly demeanor allows students to approach him and open up easily.

2. *There Is No Lesson That Can't Be Improved Upon*: Prescribed lessons directly from textbooks usually need to be tailored to meet students' needs. Bob notices, "I rewrite most lessons – put it in PowerPoint and source it. I supplement beyond the text, because I don't think the text does a good enough job illustrating things for kids." When Bob teaches, he makes adjustments, class-by-class, depending on student

comprehension. For instance, if a compound sentence confuses student understanding, Bob will break it into two separate sentences. While changes like this may seem small in scale, this attention-to-detail provides enormous benefits. Bob also makes copies of his PowerPoint presentation for his students so that they can focus on learning as opposed to note taking.

Over the years, Bob has paid close attention to the pacing of his lessons. He is keen on chunking his lessons – breaking them into two instead of one – so that students truly digest what is taught. Bob also includes activities to support his lessons and maintain students' attention.

3. *"Kaizen" – Continuous Improvement*: In *Mind Gym*, Gary Mack and David Casstevens, two sports psychologists, write about techniques to help elite athletes build mental muscle. The Japanese term, *kaizen*, was highlighted, because it focuses on practices for continuous improvement. Bob said that when he read this book, it made so much sense. Even though it was written for athletes, he learned a lot as a coach and teacher. Bob says, "You can never be done learning." With all the advances in technology and changes in education, teachers must demonstrate a willingness to enhance their skill sets through whatever means.

Even though Bob is a senior in terms of age, he remains intellectually curious and strives to stay current. He does so by attending conferences, speaking with university professors, and learning from his students. In discussing tenure and the difference between a teacher with ten years versus someone with one year of experience, Bob replies, "There's a difference having ten years of experience versus one year of experience ten times." In other words, every year should be different with ten years. Bob asks, "If you do the lesson ten times, is that really growth?" What does Bob do? He answers, "I really try to make every year different with my practice and lessons…with technology…teaching through stories…change it every year. Don't get in a velvet rut and do the same old, same old."

4. _Customize Lessons for Your Students and Area_: As much as possible, teachers need to personalize education and move away from standard fare. Customization results in strong connections that substantially and efficiently accelerate learning. At his school, Bob takes advantage of his school's 22-acre arboretum that he cultivates as his outside classroom. With over 145 different species of trees, his science lessons bloom, grabbing hold of student interest. There is a half-mile walking trail which takes kids to four native grass plots (demonstrating the original prairies found in Nebraska), a running waterfall, a man-made pond, and a water garden full of fish. By combining his depth of historical knowledge of the area with folksy, yet scientific storytelling, Bob makes learning fun, unique, and completely authentic as opposed to just studying from a textbook.

5. _Show Wonder and Awe as a Learner_: When all of the 2011 Teachers of the Year were asked to write five words to describe a good teacher, the word passionate appeared the most often. Bob states, "It wasn't about content. It was the people part of teaching…passion for the subject, kids, and learning." In teaching young people, Bob encourages other teachers to show and share their excitement with their students. "That enthusiasm spreads to the kids," says Bob. For instance, Bob's students in his field biology class collected ten different insect species. As they examined tortoise beetles and hairy beetles under

the microscope, everyone, including the teacher, shared in the wonder and awe of nature. As a former student once said to Bob, "I don't remember any of the biology you taught me, but I remember your passion."

## Other Interview Questions

*1. Who is/are your role model(s) from an educational perspective?*

In Bob's family, there are three generations of teachers, including his mom, daughter, and himself. Perhaps it is the culture for those who decide to give of themselves for the greater good. Either way, Bob's biggest role model is his mother. Bob states, "My mom was a classroom teacher in one-room schools in Nebraska for 35 years. She actually began teaching when she was 18!" What made Bob's mom such a special teacher, in his perspective, is her ability to share and give. "She just adopted her students like my brother and me. And, sometimes she treated them better than my brother and me!" laughs Bob. Most importantly, she demonstrated a willingness to sacrifice her time and put forth energy for her students.

*2. When you take a look at teachers, in general, and recognize all the hard work and devotion they put into their jobs, what would you say is the one thing that you think teachers can improve upon so they can become more highly effective?*

"No matter how hard you are working, or think you are working, you can still do more!" says Bob. The way that he maintains his high intensity work ethic is that Bob truly loves what he does. Therefore, it has become a lifestyle, and not a burden. It is true that finding balance is difficult. However, Bob's love has always been about the school, his students, and taking care of the trees in the arboretum.

In fact, many of Bob's hobbies, such as collecting rocks, finding artifacts, and birding, are directly correlated to his profession as a science teacher. So, the moral of the story is to match one's personal interests closely with the subject-matter in order to teach students effectively.

*3. Are there policies that your school (or past school) has adopted which allow teachers to excel?*

At his school, teachers are compensated for attending professional development over the summer. Bob comments, "They are paying stipends for summer workshop attendance now, though at about half salary, but it used to not be compensated at all!" This has been a motivating factor for some teachers. That said, Bob believes that a reward system to compel teachers to partake in learning opportunities may not be the best solution. An intrinsic motivation to become a better educator is what is needed the most.

*4. In order to improve our educational system, what are the shortcomings you notice in schools. What are some of the good things happening? What do you think needs to change?*

Bob identifies a number of shortcomings, including not enough professional development, technology, and collaboration. At the same time, he believes that there is too much mandated testing.

Even though schools may have professional development opportunities, it is not always mandated that teachers attend. Bob believes that many educators would benefit from learning from others and keeping up-to-date. "If you are running pages out of a publisher's workbook, that's just not the way to teach today…things are changing so fast…if you're not out there in the fray, how can you teach the kids what's contemporary?" asks Bob. As Bob likes to say, "They need to get out of the velvet rut."

In terms of technology, there are so many new applications, via software, hardware, and Internet, to reach different kinds of learners. Schools need to invest in this aspect of education, even though school monies are limited. At Bob's school, there are 20 computers for 250 students at the technology lab. Bob sees this as severely inadequate. There needs to be a way, unlike how it is currently done, to raise additional capital for schools.

Opportunities to collaborate must increase. Bob states, "There is a chasm in teacher preparation programs between the college of education and that of business and technology. How kids are taught in other schools, other than education, do not model very well." In the classroom, the Teachers of the Year could and should serve as a resource to model effective teaching for others. Cross-curricular collaboration should also be encouraged. However, No Child Left Behind has forced teachers to focus on high-stakes testing for their specific subject instead of collaborating with their peers.

As for the good things happening, the recognition that early childhood education is highly correlated to future student achievement is good. Bob declares, "Our district just started a pre-school this year. Early childhood learning is a key to educational success." Citing research from the Center of Public Policy, Bob states, "College educated parents' three-year olds will know 3,000 vocabulary words by the time they're three. Non-college educated parents' three-year olds will only know 1,500. So, will that playing field ever get level for those kids? You've got to accelerate the learning." Poverty is a driving factor and low income families do not have the financial wherewithal to expose their children to an external environment where they can supplement what is learned at home. That, as well as many other reasons, is why early childhood education is so very important.

According to Bob, there are a number of areas that require change. First, teacher professional development needs to increase. Next, there must be a higher level of commitment on the part of teachers, administrators, and school boards. Lastly, the "traditional model" of what a school is and does needs to change.

To his last point, Bob refers to the work of well-known educationalist, Sir Ken Robinson, who promotes a culture of creativity. The linear progression of elementary students based on chronological age does not necessarily make sense. Bob states, "A third grader age-wise might be a fifth grader math-wise. So you leave them in a third grade classroom....That makes no sense. We have to break that model." The model that Bob likes is a project-based learning environment, known as a Learning Studio, promoted by the National Commission on Teaching & America's Future. About four to six teachers work collaboratively in interdisciplinary, cross-curricular teams to instruct 50 to 60 students. There is no separate math class. Instead, it is sort of like a gym. There is a science corner, an English corner, and so forth. Bob describes, "You break, huddle, and come out and do lessons in the middle of the class with everyone involved. The English teacher is teaching a lesson about the science lesson. Maybe the math teacher is doing something about the conversion of metric system." Everyone is involved in the process and knows what everyone else is doing. The walls that separate are broken down. "The world is an integrated place," says Bob. That is how education should be taught.

# CHAPTER 17

## Myrra Lee

1977 National Teacher of the Year

(Social Living, U.S. History, Women's Studies – Grades 9 to 12)

*"Teaching is involvement."*

*—Myrra Lee*

For every generation, newfangled pedagogies appear to enhance learning in the classroom. No matter what a teacher's philosophy is, Myrra Lee distills education in its most essential form, stating, "Teaching is involvement." It is so because she says, "[M]ost teachers would agree that the one purpose of education is to produce functioning, self-reliant human beings who can translate their academic experience into a foundation for purposeful adulthood." That is why

Myrra utilized and endorses simulations in the classroom as one important teaching technique. While simulations of authentic real-world experiences translated into the classroom may take more time to plan and prepare, its ability to engage students and produce positive learning outcomes are well worth it.

The origin of Myrra's philosophy to involve students began with her exposure to the Socratic Method. Myrra believes that teaching and learning needed to involve the entire person. Students learn best when they become involved, and have a vested interest in what is being taught. For Myrra, this is most effectively accomplished by non-traditional methods of teaching such as simulations which replicate authentic learning. "Simulations deal with the emotional, imaginative and creative aspects of students' minds. Simulations touch students in ways that a book or lecture cannot. They open up learning possibilities that traditional methods have enclosed," declares Myrra. In addition, students tend to retain what they learn from simulations as opposed to rote memorization. Myrra points out, "People forget 80% of what they memorize. Devised methods that allow students to be creative help kids how to think."

## Background

Even though education was highly valued in her family, Myrra never intended to become a teacher. However, it was a work-related experience that compelled Myrra to pursue teaching. After college, Myrra took a secretary position at a large Veterans Affairs hospital. Myrra recounts, "While there, I had contact with many adults whose lives had little or no direction. Slowly, there evolved within me the perception of what teaching could be. Perhaps it would be possible to avert the tragic lives which surrounded me. I applied to Teacher's

College…and prepared for the teaching career which has played a major role in my life."

For over 30 years, Myrra dedicated herself as an advocate for equity and human civil rights. Due to her activist work in teaching young women and underrepresented groups, Myrra Lee is one of the pioneers in social education. She taught high school students in social living, United States history, and women's studies at Helix High School in La Mesa, California. Most important to Myrra, she taught her students how to think, feel, and form their own opinions through active participation. Myrra asserts, "As teachers, we cannot be simply imparters of information. We cannot be disseminators of morals and values. We must provide the means by which students develop the ability to recognize their values, evaluate them in the light of their ethical implications, and accept or reject them on that basis." Her teaching methods have always been original and creative, rarely resembling the instruction of others. As a strong proponent of authentic learning, Myrra utilized in-class simulations of real-world events to teach.

Due to her leading role in women's education and teaching of young people, Myrra earned numerous awards and recognitions. She was named the 1977 National Teacher of the Year and California State Teacher of the Year. Myrra was also awarded the first annual Susan B. Anthony Award from the National Organization of Women for her work. In addition, she is a Fulbright Scholar recipient. Aside from teaching, Myrra has published numerous articles on the use of simulations in the classroom and *Teaching About Women in History*. Today, Myrra is retired, but remains active in her community and with local and national organizations.

Myrra received her bachelor's degree in American institutions at the University of Wisconsin and her master's in education at Teacher's College, Columbia University.

## Teacher Top 5

1. *Competence, Competence, Competence*: In many ways, students learn only as much as a teacher can teach them. Thereafter, it is up to the teacher to guide them independently so that students can meet and exceed their full potential. Myrra believes that teachers must know their subject-matter intimately. They also need to think deeply how to present material effectively to reach every student. Myrra states, "Teachers must understand that people learn in different ways. Male brains are different from female brains." That is why Myrra advocates Howard Gardner's Multiple Intelligences Theory. It articulates that there are differences among individuals in the way they learn, and identifies strengths that each person may possess. The challenge, of course, is to figure this out for each pupil. Therefore, educators need to know their students well. On the whole, teacher competence is quite broad. At its most base level, it encapsulates attributes from subject-matter expertise, recognizing different learning styles, practicing Multiple Intelligences Theory, delivering instruction effectively, and knowing students so well that optimal learning takes place.

2. *Teacher Confidence*: Confidence allows a certain level of openness and risk-taking in a classroom. It means not only being secure as an individual and knowing the material taught, but also creating a classroom where student thoughts, perspectives, and experiences will be respected, and not breached and judged. Those educators

who possess and practice confidence can create a nurturing and safe environment where everyone feels comfortable participating.

In her Women's Studies class, Myrra practiced and advocated such confidence. Normally taboo and sensitive topics like sexual abuse, rape, and suicide were discussed. Myrra states, "In sharing experiences and perspectives, it was understood that nothing said goes outside of the classroom." In conjunction with the aforementioned topics, Myrra also invited guest speakers and experts to participate in their discussions. Teacher confidence goes a long way to enhance student learning beyond a traditional class.

3. _Develop Trust_: In many non-college preparatory classes such as Social Living and Women's Studies, learning comes from discussions among everyone in the classroom. Topics are usually sensitive such sex education in Social Living and molestation in Women's Studies. In order to compel students to lend their voices, teachers must develop mutual trust between teacher and student as well as student and student. Myrra states, "Trust opens kids up to talk seriously about sensitive issues." How do you develop trust? Myrra knows that it does not happen on the first day of class. Rather, teachers must practice and model what is expected, demonstrating honesty, openness, caring, and a willingness to share themselves. In some ways, teachers who know how to develop trust live and breathe it on a daily basis. That is important because students are perceptive and can quickly figure out, whether a teacher is truly trustworthy or not.

4. _Respect for Students_: "Most people live up or down to the expectations you set for them," says Myrra. As a classroom teacher, it is imperative that teachers have high expectations of their students

and give them the due respect that is deserved. This way, all learners can fulfill their potential. Human beings have a high capacity to learn and young people, in particular, are enormously creative and imaginative. Myrra recognizes that bridging the capacity of learning and creativity means fostering a belief that students can accomplish anything. Myrra confesses, "I know they [students] can do things." That is why she pushes students hard and holds them accountable.

5. _Enthusiasm for Teaching_: When Myrra entered Teachers College at Columbia University in the 1950s, she discovered that the bottom 10% of graduating seniors from respective undergraduate programs went on to become teachers. Myrra states, "People went into teaching for security." She, on the other hand, saw teaching as a service to humanity. Myrra embraced students as companions, traveling together on a journey to learn. She was excited to teach young people. She believes that one of the keys to being a successful teacher is to love what you do. Myrra proclaims, "There should be an electric quality in your classroom. You should be excited about what you're doing. You must have passion for teaching." In fact, teacher enthusiasm should be apparent and authentic. Those who embody this can easily get students enthusiastic about learning too.

**Other Interview Questions**

_1. Who is/are your role model(s) from an educational perspective?_

As a pioneer in social education, Myrra developed her personal teaching style over 30 years of teaching and created her subject-matter material on her own. Since there were not many educators exploring social sciences involving Women's Studies, Social Living, and minority roles in United States history, Myrra states that there were not many role models to guide her.

*2. When you take a look at teachers, in general, and recognize all the hard work and devotion they put into their jobs, what would you say is the one thing that you think teachers can improve upon so they can become more highly effective?*

Since every student learns differently, Myrra believes that students should be assessed and evaluated cognitively when they first come to school. Myrra states, "Students should be tested when they come to school. What type of learner are you? All types are equally valid." This way, teachers know what resonates with their students beforehand. It allows teachers to craft their instruction and alter their teaching style to meet the needs of their students. Myrra sees the past behavioral approach to teaching as antiquated and unrealistic. Teaching should be individualized and not a one-size-fits-all schematic.

*3. Are there policies that your school (or past school) has adopted which allow teachers to excel?*

First and foremost, allowing freedom and creativity for teachers are paramount. Myrra believes that high-stakes testing has handcuffed many school systems. Many times, the most effective way to teach is to trust teachers and permit them to reach children the best way they know how. Myrra advocates for authentic learning such as the use of simulation as a great technique to reach students. For instance, Myrra expanded a simulation activity for the 1965 Watts Riots. She created several communities, comprised of students, to portray people of different socio-economic and racial groups. Myrra states, "The goal was for students to understand what the Watts Riots were about from multiple perspectives, while studying Black history in the United States."

*4. In order to improve our educational system, what are the shortcomings you notice in schools. What are some of the good things happening? What do you think needs to change?*

Myrra believes that schools are having a difficult time understanding how to tap a student's full potential. Without knowing how to do this, a young person's cognitive development will be modest at best. Currently, there is too much emphasis on standards-based assessments. "We need to teach skills, not to the test," says Myrra. In addition, educators should be teaching students how to think so that they can acquire the skills they need to be meaningful contributors to society.

A common theme found in letters addressed to Myrra from students is, "She taught me how to think, not what to think." Myrra states, "That is the greatest compliment a teacher can receive. And that, ultimately, is what education should achieve."

# CHAPTER 18

## Roy Hudson
Alabama State Teacher of the Year (2009)
(Theater – Grades 9 to 12)

*"What a child can do in collaboration today, he can do alone tomorrow."*

— *Lev Vygotsky*

Education is a profession where teachers give students the skills, abilities, and technologies to accomplish tasks. Roy states, "We help students with those tasks, when they need our help. We challenge them above what they can do...eventually, they grab the brass ring. Together, we're designing their education." Ultimately, the objective is for students to grow independent of teachers so that they can problem solve on their own. This is especially the case in the performing arts, Roy's subject-area of teaching, and why Vygotsky resonates.

Often known as the "Mozart of Psychology," Lev Vygotsky is a titan in the fields of child development and education. Even though Vygotsky passed away nearly 80 years ago, his theory of the zone of proximal development[1] is timeless. "There is a strong repetition of Vygotsky's quote [in my *Teacher Top 5*]…that's pretty much how I approach education," says Roy.

In theatre, performers initially walk on stage singularly. Every artist brings his or her talents, experiences, and passion. As a company, everyone joins together to become one. Roy quotes, "A thousand candles can be lit from a single candle. The life of the candle will never be shortened by sharing its light." He adds, "It's collaboration and that's what we do. We work together, not by ourselves….That's what a production is about."

## Background

Every person's path to education is different, and Roy Hudson's journey is no exception. Prior to full-time public school teaching, Roy was involved in almost every aspect of theatre arts for about 20 years. He played the roles of actor, director, producer, playwright, and designer. The body of Roy's work was seen on television, film, theatre, and commercials. In fact, Roy even ran his own freelance design and production company. You name it, and Roy has done it in the performing arts.

All that said, it was Shades Valley High School's lucky day when Roy decided to become a teacher as a way of giving back as well as sharing his expertise and enthusiasm with young people. Over the course of his 15-year teaching career, Roy transformed the high school theatre program into a critically-acclaimed and award winning Shades Valley Theatre Academy. As one of the top theatre schools in the Southeast, Roy's productions were often recognized as Best of Show in state competitions and Southeastern Theatre Conference and International Thespian Society. For his many accomplishments, Roy was named 2009 Alabama State Teacher of the Year. Roy's awards and honors also include, but are not limited to, United States Department of Education Teacher Leader for the State of Alabama, Kennedy Center Outstanding Direction for *Band Geeks!*, and Alabama Educational Theatre Association Hall of Fame Award.

In addition to teaching, Roy is very active in the community. He helped co-found STARS (Students Take a Role at the Samford), a regional educational outreach program for children. He also served as theatre supervisor to the Jefferson Board of Education. Today, Roy serves as the Artistic Director and Director of Educational Programs at the Virginia Samford Theatre in Birmingham, Alabama.

Roy received his bachelor's degree in education from Midwestern State University. He also holds a master's degree in theatre from Trinity University. At the University of Alabama at Birmingham, Roy graduated summa cum laude with a master's in education.

## Teacher Top 5

1. *It Is Our Children's Education – Not Ours*: "It's very important for students to know what's happening and why they're doing and

approaching things a certain way," says Roy. That way, "Students can say, 'Oh, I get it. This is why we're doing this.'" As a teacher, Roy tries to share as much as he can with his students. He states, "We must involve them in every aspect of the educational process so that they understand that they have a level of control for what and how they learn."

Every student's education must also be tailored to fit his or her needs. Having taught English, literature, and writing as well as theatre, Roy is known for creating an individualized plan for each student. He declares, "It's not as hard as it sounds. For example, if a student in my writing class is a whiz at grammar, but his writing lacks style or impact, then we work on style and impact. If, on the other hand, another student has remarkable writing abilities and style, but does not consistently use correct grammar, then we work on his grammar." All students must be treated fairly, but each person has strengths and weaknesses. It is up to the teacher to evaluate and determine what each child's strength is, and what still needs further work.

2. _Employ Educational Scaffolding in Every Classroom_: In education, scaffolding is used to describe the support provided to a student by a teacher. Scaffolding relates closely to Vygotsky's theory of the zone of proximal development, because it helps maintain a student's potential level of development. Roy is well aware that independence is the ultimate goal. For this reason, scaffolding must exist in all instruction. Roy asserts, "Always challenge students with projects or assignments that they can accomplish with help and move them to a point, if possible, where they can complete their work independently." Scaffolding can take many forms. In theatre, Roy models everything for students so they have an example as a reference. He states, "I'm

a visual person. I try to model everything and don't just give oral instruction." Thereafter, students can review and practice. While scaffolding is effective in the performing arts, it is also applicable to all subjects, including math and language arts.

3. *Utilize Project-Based Learning Whenever Possible*: Roy raves, "While designing these projects takes time, the results can be incredible as students solve problems and explore the world in an attempt to complete the project." There are generational differences in how young people learn, think, and play. Roy notices that, today, students figure things out as they go, as opposed to needing to know the rules first. The beauty of project-based learning is that problems exist which require solutions that touch on multiple disciplines.

For instance, Roy taught an Introduction to Theatre class which exposed students to the craft. He created a student group project to interpret *Romeo & Juliet*. A team of three students took on the responsibilities of director, set designer, and costume designer. Students were required to pick a historical period and translate Shakespeare's work. Instead of the 1400s, the time period could have been the Civil Rights era. Romeo might be African American and Juliet could be White. Students would perform research, modernize the literature, create renderings for the set, write a paper on their work, and present their material in a comprehensive fashion to their peers. The power of projects is that they encompass multiple disciplines, including social studies, writing, math, art, and so forth. Roy adds, "This is really where educational scaffolding works the best."

4. *Collaboration is a Key Element for Student Success*: Collaboration allows students to learn from each other and develop skills they

would not normally learn from working by themselves. Roy declares, "Anytime that you can create a situation where students work together on a project or an assignment, they develop the social skills they need to be successful in all aspects of their lives." In fact, collaboration promotes life skills that students can take with them long after they leave the school setting. Roy points out the importance of collaboration by recounting the words of the great swimmer, Michael Phelps, after his final competition at the Olympics. When asked by Bob Costas what his most satisfying win was, Phelps immediately identified the relays because of the camaraderie amongst his teammates. "By collaborating, you bring out the best in everybody," says Roy.

5. _Create a Classroom that is Safe, Inviting, and Promotes Questions_: First and foremost, teachers need to recognize that school is not just about them. Rather, it is all about the students. On day one, teachers must be inclusive of students. Young people must know what they say is important, and they will not be ridiculed for their responses. Student contribution is essential and everybody takes part, not only a few key students. Roy states, "If a child feels safe to question and explore, then he or she will. Everything else will fall into place, if this one simple element is employed."

When people ask Roy what are his classroom rules, Roy replies, "I only have one. It's respect. You respect yourself, classmates, and teacher. The teacher must also respect the students." This mutual respect must exist so that effective collaboration can take place. Roy continues, "Teachers are facilitators…gone are the days when everyone sits at a tree, students gather around, and the teacher imparts knowledge."

## Other Interview Questions

*1. Who is/are your role model(s) from an educational perspective?*

Roy looks up to Lev Vygotsky and Nancie Atwell for their educational thought leadership and contributions. Roy states, "Vygotsky was the one who first outlined the educational philosophy of instructional scaffolding...while he didn't [actually use the term scaffolding], all of the principles are there." Nancie Atwell, a very highly respected American educator, is perhaps best known for her reading and writing workshop approach, chronicled in her book, *In the Middle.* Roy points out, "When [Atwell] wrote about her work in writing, she applied many of Vygotsky's principles in a very easy-to-use way for American students." He adds, "I think everything she writes is brilliant and the way she sets up her class is the way it should be." Her work is especially compelling, because she applied it in her own classroom and experienced success 20 to 30 years ago. Lastly, Roy notes that Vygotsky and Atwell's philosophies were not embraced by everyone initially, and even now there are skeptics. That said, their philosophies definitely resonate with Roy.

*2. When you take a look at teachers, in general, and recognize all the hard work and devotion they put into their jobs, what would you say is the one thing that you think teachers can improve upon so they can become more highly effective?*

"There are too many teachers who have never been anything but teachers...they may be incredibly effective imparting the basic tenets of their subject matter...[however]...if they have little experience applying these principles in authentic situations, then they are not truly reaching their students," says Roy. In his own professional career, Roy was involved in almost every facet of performing arts before becoming a theatre teacher. At 42 years of age, Roy delved into teaching after gaining substantial real-world experience that he could impart to students.

Roy continues, "We must prepare our students to become self-sufficient not only in the process of learning, but also in the application of what they have learned so that they can provide for themselves and become competitive in a ever-changing and frighteningly competitive job market. We must find a way to give our teachers authentic experiences in their subject-matter so that they can make their lessons and the skills they are teaching relevant. We need to develop plans to bring professionals who are using these skills in their jobs into classrooms to work with our students and to challenge and mentor them."

*3. Are there policies that your school (or past school) has adopted which allow teachers to excel?*

Roy loves the concept of academic academies which are focused on art, theatre, engineering, finance, and a variety of trades such as automotive and HVAC. Students are given the opportunity "to apply their education in authentic situations." Academic academies have been instituted and blossomed at many school districts. Within a school, these academies solicit students who show a particular interest in a subject-area. Then, they are taught by experienced and highly motivated teachers. Students intern at businesses and organizations, and they have school work associated with it.

As a results-oriented educator, Roy states, "Our ultimate goal for K through 12 is to get kids to college, or get them in a position to get a job." He adds, "Prior to the creation of the Theatre Academy in 2001, my students rarely had the opportunity to work in the various pro-fessional theatre companies in the area. After that time, I was given the support to change that. The scholarships offered to my students to attend colleges and universities saw a dramatic increase…for the next ten years, my students averaged more than a million dollars in scholarship monies each year for a graduating class of approximately twelve students."

*4. In order to improve our educational system, what are the shortcomings you notice in schools. What are some of the good things happening? What do you think needs to change?*

The Pearson/Smithsonian collaboration and charter school initia-tive are two positive areas of education. Roy declares, "The Pearson Foundation, in collaboration with the Smithsonian Institute, has…a project to develop digital and mobile technology lessons. Utilizing an incredible number of workshops with both leading educators and students, they have created and tested these plans in actual class-rooms across the country with remarkable results. These project-based lessons encompass all content areas and all grade levels."

Roy goes on, "I think the continued development of the charter school initiative is another positive attempt to improve our schools. In Louisiana, the charter schools that moved into New Orleans after Hurricane Katrina have already made incredible strides with Title I schools….Alabama is piloting several new Charter Schools this fall in three inner city school systems. This is the first time for our state, and I hope that the results approach what is happening in New Orleans."

In terms of change, Roy calls attention to the education of both the low income students in the inner city and rural areas, as well as the academically gifted students across the country. He states, "One of the suggestions that I think would help all schools is to develop a year-round school calendar. Every study done has shown that this will improve test scores in all areas. Our school calendar is still based on an agrarian population. That is just not the case anymore, and we need to abandon it."

Roy continues, "In reality, we need to reexamine all elements of our schools and look at them from the perspective of the 21st century. Students should advance by subject area, not necessarily by a grade that groups all subjects together. Let students move forward and challenge them in the subjects where they excel while remediating them in those where they need additional time and/or help. Embrace the digital era and organize schools, classes, school work and projects to utilize digital and mobile technology in substantive ways."

# CHAPTER 19

**Jason Hughes**
West Virginia State Teacher of the Year (2005)
(Agriculture – Grades 9 to 12)

*"I am not a teacher of subject-matter, but a teacher of students."*
*— Anonymous*

While the author of this quote is unknown, Jason Hughes uses it often and has heard it repeated by others on special occasions. His affinity for the quote stems from his belief that students come first. Period. Jason states, "It's a quote to keep your job in perspective. Keep the kids first, and the subject-matter will take care of itself."

Teaching is so much more than simply delivering instruction. Rather, it is about caring for students and guiding them through their path in life. "I tell my students that I love them, and I mean it. My students are the reason that I teach. I love the challenge of trying to shape their minds and personalities through my teaching and influence," explains Jason. He continues, "You are trying to teach students to be good people and good citizens. I want them to be productive citizens."

Needless to say, Jason is a teacher who embraces the whole child. He declares, "I'm not an agriculture teacher. I'm not a math teacher. I'm a teacher of students." This holistic approach is interwoven throughout his philosophy of teaching. A philosophy that takes into consideration the needs of all students and helps each person find his or her individual calling.

**Background**

Some people are simply called to teach, and that is how it was for Jason Hughes. It is his calling in life. Wherever he goes, teaching is front and center. Jason not only teaches at school, but he is also very active in his church and within the community. Perhaps it is because teaching is in his family genes. His family tree includes educators such as his great grandfather, grandfather, uncles, and aunts. Jason shares, "I am very proud to continue the family tradition of teaching."

For Jason, teaching agricultural science has afforded him the opportunity to pursue his two greatest passions: making a difference in the lives of others, and passing on his love of agriculture and the environment. While teaching at St. Marys High School, Jason developed two very unique courses, Hydroponics and Agricultural Biotechnology. Both classes were oversubscribed and provided advanced exposure to the scientific field of agriculture. With his students, Jason also established a free countywide water-testing program. Water was tested for more than 50 local residents. Thereafter, results were mailed back to the participants. Outside of the classroom, one of the Jason's biggest accomplishments was founding the Pleasants County Agricultural Youth Fair in 2000. The fair now attracts hundreds of youth exhibitors and Future Farmers of America ("FFA") members. It also provides entertainment like wood chop contests, livestock shows, and pedal tractor pulls.

For his commitment and hard work in education, Jason has been recognized by numerous organizations. In 2005, he was named West Virginia Teacher of the Year. He was also selected National FFA Honorary Member and West Virginia Agriscience Teacher of the Year. The Southern States Agricultural Leadership Award was also given to Jason for his outstanding demonstrated leadership in the agriculture education profession.

Jason received his bachelor's and master's degrees in agriculture from West Virginia University. He also holds an educational leadership certification from Salem International University.

## Teacher Top 5

1. *Care About Your Students*: Quite simply, students have to know that the teacher genuinely cares about them. Jason says, "The reason to why it's important is because kids know a fake when they see one. When they know that you sincerely care about where they're going in life, they end up wanting to work harder for you as a teacher."

Teachers can demonstrate their care by doing things beyond the classroom such as attending after-school activities and accepting student invitations to family events. "Becoming a part of their life through extracurricular activities really makes a difference," claims Jason.

Treating students like adults and with respect goes a long way. If a teacher is successful in developing a strong student-teacher relationship, former students will keep in touch long after they graduate. Jason shares, "Several years ago, a student who I still keep in touch with called me to ask for my advice about a job he was thinking about taking. At the end of the call, he also asked me to be the best man for his wedding." This shows the power of connections and the impact teachers have on young people.

2. _Set the Context for Students_: All too often when students are introduced to new material, teachers hear the questions, "Why do I need to know this?" and "How does this relate to my life?" As a teacher, Jason states, "I make sure that I put into context whatever they are learning so they don't have to ask those questions…if kids don't understand why they're learning it, they'll shut down." Teachers also need to make connections that are cross-curricular and cross-subjects.

As an example, math can often be a subject-matter that is difficult to embrace and easy to lose interest. In teaching agricultural science, Jason embeds math into his activities and lessons. If students are tasked with sowing seeds in the greenhouse and asked to calculate germination rates, they must use math to figure out how many plants they will have and how that would fit in their packaging. "They're learning math, but in a context that makes it simpler. It's much different than taking out a book and then performing 20 problems," states Jason. Activities must have purpose, connect to real life, and be meaningful to their everyday lives.

3. _Drive for Students to be Engaged_: It is essential to create an environment where students engage in their own learning and the teacher acts as a guide. This can be accomplished by developing a thoughtful, project-based class as opposed to pure lecturing and reading. When Jason first taught his Hydroponics class which focused on growing plants in water, he could have easily turned to a text laden with information. Instead, Jason required student teams to design and build their own hydroponic system for growing plants. Thereafter, students were asked to present their hydroponic system to members of the State Department of Education and County Offices. Newspaper articles about what students were doing in class ensued. Ultimately, this proved to be enormously rewarding for students as they pushed to learn everything about this field of study. "Make students participants with you [in the learning process]…it shouldn't be one-sided delivery where the teacher instructs and students listen. Engage students to help them take ownership of their own learning. Let them make mistakes and allow them to theorize. Great learning happens in this type of environment," declares Jason.

4. _Promote High Expectations_: Students rise to the level set for them and perform to where teachers would like them to be. To create this type of environment, it starts with effective teacher communication. Jason states, "It's what you say, and constantly reinforce. Consistency is critical. You must hold everyone accountable at the same level. You must be fair and balanced…and you must stay on your message." When students are with him, Jason communicates messages like:

"If you are going to do something, do it right;" "Treat people well;" "Do a quality job;" "Be ambitious and go after what you want;" and "Don't have any regrets." Consequences are also important and must be reinforced. Sometimes, it can take the form of written contracts to address behavior, commitment of time, and so forth. By doing all of this, Jason says, "You create a culture, and students who take your class know what to expect."

5. _Constantly Evaluating and Re-evaluating One's Effectiveness as a Teacher_: "Professional growth is so important…to find out what's working and what's not," declares Jason. Without it, it is difficult to become a better educator. Jason suggests performing reflection, whether it is formal or informal. It can be done daily, weekly, monthly, or at the end of the school year. Jason states, "Look at your course of instruction, expose the weak areas of content, and find what you need to do to shore that area up." If stronger content knowledge is needed, then seek professional development opportunities like seminars and hands-on labs. If technical equipment would help, then perform grant writing. Either way, there should be an action item associated with each identified issue. "Reflection without action is pointless. Be honest with yourself," asserts Jason. "Take the initiative and seek out professional development. Don't sit back and be told by others."

**Other Interview Questions**

_1. Who is/are your role model(s) from an educational perspective?_

"I feel blessed to have had some excellent teachers throughout my educational journey," states Jason. For example, Mrs. Cales, his fourth grade teacher, was an exceptional educator. Her compassion and love for her students came across easily and touched everyone she taught. Mr. Morgan, his fifth grade teacher, was Jason's first exposure to a male educator. Jason shares, "This opened my eyes [at that age] that males can be teachers. Being able to interact with him differently compared to female teachers was a really nice experience." Mr. Morgan set high expectations and cared about his students in a benign manner. Jason said that both Mrs. Cales and Mr. Morgan were hard and did not "baby" their students. At the same time, Jason tells, "Everyone knew they loved us." Lastly, Jason's two high school agriculture teachers, Mr. Stephens and Mr. Burdette, were highly influential. Jason notes how they made learning fun, authentic, and engaging.

*2. When you take a look at teachers, in general, and recognize all the hard work and devotion they put into their jobs, what would you say is the one thing that you think teachers can improve upon so they can become more highly effective?*

Being proactive is a big part of what teachers can do to become more highly effective. Since teachers are so bogged down with their day-in and day-out teaching as well as policies from state and county boards, cynicism can creep in quickly. "Look what they're doing to us," says Jason, is an often heard complaint from teachers. To reverse that, Jason encourages, "Take control of your own destiny." He adds, "Change your mindset. Don't wait to be told what to do. Seek out your own professional growth. Be self-motivated to do it."

*3. Are there policies that your school (or past school) has adopted which allow teachers to excel?*

"It's all trickle down," declares Jason. When the leader of a school embraces high expectations, the school will promote a culture that has many of the *Teacher Top 5* traits discussed earlier. Teachers will rise to the occasion and flourish. Jason states, "Iron sharpens iron. When good strong teachers are able to rub elbows with others, they become better teachers….That's my philosophical viewpoint."

Administration can often be the key for teacher success or failure. Teachers work very hard. However, administration can often be challenging due to the lack of teacher support or uninspired leadership. Jason points out, "I've even heard teachers say they're going to quit teaching, because of administration. Therefore, I know it's a problem." To remedy this, Jason suggests creating a school culture of excellence with high expectations, discipline, and structure. This way, teachers feel supported.

*4. In order to improve our educational system, what are the shortcomings you notice in schools. What are some of the good things happening? What do you think needs to change?*

Aside from teaching, teachers are so loaded up with extra responsibilities that it stifles their creativity. Jason asserts, "It also stifles their time for reflection." Time is arguably the biggest shortcoming that teachers do not have, but need. "We have to have time for professional growth and reflection….How do you make things better? You reflect and then tap into your creativity," states Jason. In addition, Jason declares, "Leadership is critical….Until the school's principal can be the true instructional leader he or she is supposed to be, and not a manager of everything, change will be difficult. Principals need to dedicate themselves more to instruction and professional growth of teachers." That said, Jason recognizes that principals are pulled in all directions, and their time and energy are limited. As a possible solution, Jason believes that the head of a school job should be split in two: an operations manager and an instructional leader.

Jason believes that there are many good things happening in schools that needs more coverage in the media. First, the majority of teachers really care about their students and they do everything they can to educate, help, and assist. Second, Jason has been very impressed with the young people entering teaching. They appear proactive and impatient, in a good way, to enact positive change. Jason states, "They care. They're proactive and want to set the world on fire." Lastly, there is a lot of instructional transition taking place such as Common Core. Jason notes, "There is a recognition that all classrooms need to be set up to engage. Instruction must be contextualized….There is a transition now." While there is much to do and change, it is slowly moving in a positive direction.

# CHAPTER 20

## George Goodfellow
Rhode Island State Teacher of the Year (2008)
(Chemistry – Grade 11)

*"If you want to build a ship, don't drum up people to collect wood and don't assign them to tasks and work, but rather teach them to long for the endless immensity of the sea."*

*— Antoine de Saint-Exupery*

George Goodfellow knows that "you reach a kid's mind through his heart." Antoine de Saint-Exupery, the writer of *The Little Prince*, captured George's sentiments exactly in his quote above. George stresses that progress in the classroom exists from teachers inspiring students. In fact, when the spotlight is on standards and testing, student learning ceases. George says, "When you don't approach teaching students by inspiring them and having them find their own desire in the subject-matter, you shut down student creativity…the standards-based approach and high-stakes testing…is doing exactly what we didn't want it to do." He continues, "Now, it's about teaching standards, teaching subject-matter, testing material, and then evaluating the level of learning based on a standardized test. It's absolutely backwards."

A long time ago, George learned from working with elementary school teachers that the most effective educators teach the student, not the subject-matter. George exclaims, "That's absolutely right!" Even though George taught chemistry, he approached it from the student's point of view. Thereafter, he would bring in the subject. That is why George champions Howard Gardner's Multiple Intelligences Theory. It is student-centered, honing in on student strengths and putting the pupil first.

## Background

George Goodfellow is the definition of veteran teacher. Over a 40 year career, he has taught more than 5,000 students in chemistry and physics. George says, "I teach because there is no profession that can contribute to the betterment of children than does teaching….They call us teacher, rabbi, maestro, magister, doctor, but whatever they call us, we give of ourselves to betterment of existence on this planet, to the development of young people, and to the fulfillment of the dreams of the next generation."

For those lucky enough to have had George as a teacher, they were not only guaranteed a solid education, but also plenty of fun. His innovative teaching style and emphasis on making learning fun are his distinctive trademarks. In chemistry class, it was not unusual to hear George leading a song, going over important facts. Best yet, George and his students were also the beneficiary of his wife's talents. Cynthia Goodfellow, a retired middle school teacher, would often accompany George in class to assist, free-of-charge to the school. "It's like I died and gone to heaven," exclaims George of having Cynthia in his classroom. Needless to say, it was a good time all around and, not surprisingly, many of his students went on to college, majoring in chemistry and the sciences.

Numerous organizations and institutions have recognized George for his exemplary teaching. Most notably, George was named the 2008 Rhode Island State Teacher of the Year. Earlier when he taught in Massachusetts, George was a nominee for Massachusetts State Teacher of the Year. He was also inducted into the Aula Laudis Honor Society for distinguished contributions to chemistry education by Northeastern University. Today, George teaches undergraduate and graduate courses for aspiring teachers.

George received his bachelor's degree in chemistry at University of Massachusetts. He also holds a master's degree in synthetic organic chemistry from Bridgewater State College.

## Teacher Top 5

1. _Know and Respect the Culture of Your Students_: Different cultures comprehend learning in their own way. Therefore, it is imperative to keep learning authentic so that students can see its relevancy. George states, "Every lesson should impart to students the knowledge that they can use in their lives as soon as they leave the classroom." This

student-centered approach puts students first, not the lesson. For instance, teaching a lesson on density must be performed differently depending on the constituents. Students from Massachusetts will construe and internalize the subject-matter of density differently compared to school children in a Navaho Indian community in a desert location of the Southwest.

George asserts, "The point here is that one lesson based around one set of content can never be relevant to all classrooms. Lessons can only be determined by the culture of the classroom and this should be evaluated by individual school systems, teachers, and administrators with the major value coming from the opinion and knowledge of the teacher in whose classroom the lesson will be presented." George continues, "The issue is to teach students what they can perceive as valuable in their learning."

2. _Build Community_: First and foremost, it is vital to understand the culture of the community. How does it function and what works best? Next, get involved. "This means get involved with the issues in the lives of students, in the lives of the people in the community, and in the school environment," says George. As a seasoned educator, George believes that school teachers are the second most influential force in a student's life after parents. In every aspect, teachers make a difference and contribute to the development of young people.

In his own experience, George remembers taking the time to write a non-solicited, but caring letter to one of his students. This student had great promise academically and athletically, however, he had enormous difficulty with criticism of any sort. George's compassionate letter addressed the student's character flaw in a thoughtful and encouraging manner. As it would be, the student's mother got wind of it and was enormously touched and thankful that George took the time to get involved in her son's life. Beyond the teacher's subject-matter, students often need outside help to confront emotional needs. Parents are important, but oftentimes, teachers are in a unique position to reach students and compel change. George states, "Students and parents need to be aware of the fact that you care about them and are using your expertise to improve lives."

3. _Wrap the Student Around the Curriculum, Not the Curriculum Around the Student_: Customarily, curriculums exist at a school which are then taught to students. "That's not the way to teach," says George. "You start with the student....Analyze your students, know their interests and goals, their strengths and their weaknesses, and then use the curriculum for which you have responsibility to help students reach those goals...." By adopting this approach, material will be much more meaningful and student retention will be longer.

When George taught chemistry, each year was different, because the students were different. The goal was not to teach everything about chemistry. Rather, it was to take students and show them how to use chemistry to improve their lives and succeed. That is how teachers create student passion for subject-material. "That is how all classes should be taught," states George. "You should not have a standard set of curriculum concepts that every student needs to learn whether they like it or not. It should be a development of intellect in the field....Organize kids to their natural abilities and then make it fundamentally sound."

4. *Teach Students How to Think and Solve Problems*: While this may seem obvious, there is a real art to teaching and assessing what students have learned. George declares, "No matter what the subject matter, there are approaches to the solution of problems within that material." In other words, teachers who differentiate instruction by applying Multiple Intelligence Theory enable students to learn effectively based on what resonates with them the most. For example, teachers should help chemistry students who learn best via musical intelligences to think and solve problems in that manner. At the same time, George states, "[C]reate an assessment system that mirrors each student's learning. The final comment (grade) that a teacher gives a student should be an accurate measurement of all that he or she has learned." In the case above, the student who learned chemistry through musical intelligences should be assessed using sounds, rhythms, tones, or music. If a standardized test is given instead, and the student performs poorly, the student is showing that he or she cannot understand the test rather than not knowing the material. Paraphrasing Howard Gardner, George states, "People use Multiple Intelligences in the real world to solve problems." That is how educators should be teaching.

5. *Be the Leader of Your Team in the Classroom*: According to Professor John Shindler, the author of *Transformational Classroom Management*, there are a number of different teaching styles. George embraces the orchestrator style. He states, "Lead by example, by positive directions, by the equitable administration of consequences and by affirmative coaching. The goal of good teaching is the continued progress of students." Once students understand that the teacher is the leader of the team and embraces the progress of the team, George

transitions to a facilitator teaching style. In this case, students are self-directed with the teacher acting like a mentor. "When they leave your mentoring, they should have grown intellectually, emotionally, and personally, and they should be aware of this progress and their own potential for continued growth," says George.

## Other Interview Questions

*1. Who is/are your role model(s) from an educational perspective?*

The work of Howard Gardner through his Multiple Intelligences Theory has inspired numerous educators, including George. He comments, "I follow the intelligence theory of Howard Gardner. His insight into how people are able to solve problems out of their diversity has inspired most of the lessons I have conducted. Although not an educator, per se, Gardner's theory has itself educated scores of teachers."

*2. When you take a look at teachers, in general, and recognize all the hard work and devotion they put into their jobs, what would you say is the one thing that you think teachers can improve upon so they can become more highly effective?*

"Teachers must realize that they are the advocates for their students. When outside forces attempt to dictate how and what they should be doing in the classroom, teachers must not blindly follow these influences. Only the individual teacher can accurately assess the best path for the education of his or her students," says George. In other words, teachers know what is best for each student in the classroom. It's neither the parents nor the administrators. It is the classroom teacher who is teaching students daily and knows the strengths, weaknesses, and desires of every pupil. For that reason, education needs to be individualized and cannot be one-size-fits-all. George encourages all stakeholders, including politicians, school systems, and parents, to ask and allow teachers to be their student advocates.

*3. Are there policies that your school (or past school) has adopted which allow teachers to excel?*

George applauds school systems that have turned to authentic assessments and lessons. He states, "The adoption of authentic assessments and authentic lessons has given teachers direction in terms of what we should provide for students. This takes on the form of project-based lessons, senior projects, and diversity in the creation of a final evaluation for each student."

As an example, senior projects are essentially a quasi-internship in an area of a student's interest. The student pairs up with a mentor in the community and performs the duties of an assistant for the entire senior year. At the end of the academic year, the student prepares a project and presents it to a panel that performs an evaluation. The senior project is a major part of the entire formal assessment to determine graduation from high school. George says, "This is far better than taking a standardized exam to see if you graduate from high school. This is an authentic approach." Furthermore, it gives students a real-world experience so that they can make good decisions when going to college or otherwise.

*4. In order to improve our educational system, what are the shortcomings you notice in schools. What are some of the good things happening? What do you think needs to change?*

George points out, "Most teachers have little to no common planning time [with their peers]." Many times, teachers are working in a vacuum. "Common planning time is invaluable…it is something every school should have," says George. That way, teachers can collaborate and talk about what works and does not, new ways to assess, and effective ways to reach students. When Multiple Intelligences Theory appeared in the 1980s, teachers were trying to figure out how best to apply it in the classroom. Common planning time would have given teachers the space to do so. George exclaims, "Teachers are in need of training to more effectively meet the goals of students. As conditions change for the school community and for students, in general, it would be helpful if teachers could keep abreast of effective ways to adjust to these changes and learn from each other, what practices are effective, and what approaches simply do not work."

In terms of things happening in education, George comments, "In my sphere of experience, the majority of educationally-related events have been negative in recent years. Public perception, political and media initiatives, and financial decisions have, for the most part, demonstrated an incorrect and demoralizing effect on teachers in general." While people decide to become teachers to serve a greater good, the financial compensation of teachers is modest. Salaries are humble and retirement monies can be adversely affected by laws such as the Windfall Elimination Provision – the law reduces the social security benefits of workers who also have pension benefits from employment not covered by social security. George shares that it is difficult to encourage young people to become teachers unless they fully understand the ramifications of what it means financially.

As far as changes go, George states, "The reality is that, in a service occupation, productivity is most influenced by the morale of the service providers. Some individual administrators understand this tenet. Most have missed the point." He adds, "You get the most out of yourself and work hard for two reasons: one is personal pride; and the other is that somebody is going to appreciate it. If you know that's true, you'll get the best out of yourself."

# CHAPTER 21

**Philip Bigler**
National Teacher of the Year (1998)
(Humanities, History – Grade 11)

*"Civilization begins anew with each child."*

— *Midrash*

Over the course of history, a wealth of Jewish literature exists, including the Torah, also known as the first five books of the Bible. When writings were not easily understandable, rabbis of the old used something known as the Midrash, an imaginative story to explain the purpose of a written passage.

Philip Bigler chose this ancient Jewish adage as his favorite quote about education. As a teacher for over 35 years, Philip states, "Education is a process of enlightenment." Therefore, students need a sense of the past and must build upon it. Philip continues, "As an educator, I have found this statement to be both a vision of optimism as well as a dire warning…I have always seen my role as a teacher to facilitate student learning in what will be a lifelong quest for knowledge, to help ignite in them the spark of enlightenment, to motivate their interest, and to cultivate their minds."

## Background

Philip Bigler has always possessed an enormous interest in history which started in fourth grade. He states, "[I]t seemed to me that history was really a great story about real people." Growing up in Illinois, Philip marveled about the state's history and the exploration of the Mississippi River by Father Jacques Marquette and Louis Joliet. As he continued his education, he graduated from high school and found himself at a crossroads about what to major in college. Philip quips, "When I went to college, I decided that I was going to study a subject matter that I enjoyed rather than worry about getting a job. I still believe that college is a place to become educated, not employed."

Many years later, Philip is true to his word and still demonstrates the same zeal and passion for history. As a seasoned educator, Philip taught high school humanities and history for three decades. During that time period, he challenged himself by teaching 22 different subjects ranging from Middle Eastern history to Photojournalism. He even took a three-year hiatus from the classroom to serve as a historian for Arlington National Cemetery in Virginia. Philip is also the author of seven books. His most recent publication, *Teaching History in an Uncivilized World*, was released in 2012 by Apple Ridge Publishers.

As a classroom teacher, Philip was widely known for his innovative teaching methods, use of technology in the classroom, and strong commitment to his students. After his distinguished tenure as a high school teacher, Philip became the director of the James Madison Center for Liberty & Learning at James Madison University. The Madison Center is devoted to improving the quality of teaching while advancing academic excellence. Philip was responsible for all aspects of the Madison Center, including academic research, public relations, and teacher training. He also continues to teach in both the history and education departments at the University.

Philip has been recognized by, and won awards from, numerous organizations, including the Distinguished Service to Education Award at George Mason University, the United States Department of Education Award for Excellence in Education, and the University of Chicago's Outstanding Teacher Award. He was also named the 1998 National Teacher of the Year.

Philip attended James Madison University where he received his bachelor's degree in history and master's degree in secondary education and history. He also earned a master's degree in American Studies from the College of William and Mary.

**Teacher Top 5**

1. *Preparation*: According to Philip, preparation is one of the most important secrets for successful teaching. No matter what grade level

or subject taught, teachers need to be well-prepared and must know their subject-matter intimately. This may mean a core competency based on past academic studies or it could simply mean having a deep knowledge of the subject from research and planning. Either way, teachers must have a strong agenda for what they will be teaching. Philip states, "Students have the most respect for educators who have an in-depth knowledge of their content."

Along the same lines, teachers need to be ready to teach once class is in session. Time is a teacher's most valuable resource and instruction should begin right away. Philip asserts, "A typical 50-minute class often is reduced to less than 30 minutes of quality instructional time by too many teachers and this is unacceptable." Teachers must convey to their students that they are ready to begin instruction immediately when the class bell sounds. Philip states, "Start into what you're doing and have high expectations [of your students]." For that reason, teachers need to plan out their day strategically to take utmost advantage of class time.

2. _Get Outside of the Classroom_: Authentic learning is the key here. Philip suggests, "Expand the classroom beyond four walls." In other words, take field trips to add excitement to the learning process. In fact, teachers should do this several times throughout the school year. That said, field trips must be content-rich and leave a lasting and memorable impact. Philip recounted a field trip to the Gettysburg battlefield which involved the entire junior class. Students not only had an incredible time, but also gained a new appreciation for history as well as for their ancestors. At the same time, he recommends, "Avoid activities that require students to fill out mindless worksheets during a field trip." The field trip chosen should be so engaging and

significant that students remain highly interested without the need for worthless busy work. Philip says, "Allow kids to rise to the occasion [and take field trips that] kids will never forget."

Another way of getting outside of the classroom is inviting meaningful guest speakers. In discussing the Vietnam War and the Gulf of Tonkin Resolution in his history class, Philip fondly remembers inviting Navy Lieutenant Everett Alvarez Jr. as a speaker. Lieutenant Alvarez is widely known as the first United States pilot shot down over North Vietnam in 1964 and held as a prisoner-of-war for nine years. Similarly, when learning about the Watergate scandal during the Nixon presidency, Philip secured Benjamin Bradlee as a guest. Mr. Bradlee was the executive editor of *The Washington Post* from 1968 to 1991. Mr. Bradlee played a pivotal role in overseeing the publication of Bob Woodward and Carl Bernstein's reports on Watergate. Speakers such as these leave indelible impressions on students many years later.

3. *Sense of Humor and Fun*: Learning should be fun. After all, the origin of the word "school" comes from the Greek word for "leisure." Philip states, "The Greeks viewed learning as a leisurely activity." Hence, bring a sense of humor to class and focus on activities that are fun. A big part of this is a teacher's personality. Teachers should share stories with their students and be able to laugh with them. Teaching should not be so serious that it feels like a chore and all of the fun is left out. Philip believes, "The best teachers enjoy what they're doing."

In studying President Calvin Coolidge, Philip enjoyed sharing a brief story about President Coolidge's "Silent Cal" reputation. During that

---

time, "Silent Cal" was notoriously known as a man of few words. While Governor of Massachusetts, Coolidge was seated at a dinner beside a Boston society woman who playfully insisted that she bet her husband $20 that Coolidge would not say even three words to her. Coolidge's response was "You lose."

4. *Know your Students Well*: First of all, there is a big difference between being friends with students versus showing care and concern for them. Teachers must keep these roles separate and remember that they are adults in a position of responsibility. After all, even teenage students are still children and in need of adult guidance. Teachers should assist them in their academic development as well as personal growth.

Philip suggests, "Know your students well." What does this mean? He states, "It's important for students to know that they're not simply a grade. They're human beings." Know each student's name; celebrate each child; ask questions; recognize them as individuals. Are they on a sports team? Do they perform in theater? How are they faring and what's happening in their lives? Philip recounted a specific example when a former student lost her cat and was deeply depressed. To show that he cared, Philip wrote a personal note, providing his heartfelt sympathy. As Philip states, "If students think you care, they care what you think." That is how teachers can get students to respond and work hard. For Philip, he would rather have students "fear my disappointment, than fear my anger."

5. *Get Up-to-Speed and Updated on Technology*: Teaching in the 21st century provides numerous opportunities to incorporate technology into the classroom. This is not simply using technology for its

own sake, but the goal is to improve the learning experience. In fact, Philip believes that if teachers are teaching the same way that they were ten years ago, then they have stagnated and failed to improve and grow as educators. From the Internet to digital resources to new and innovative software, the possibilities are limitless. For instance, PowerPoint can be an extremely effective way to convey information. It can also be used for "Back to School Night" to showcase student activities and projects for the parents. Other options include Adobe Photoshop, Serif Software, and a variety of movie-making software and applications.

Philip believes that schools must provide opportunities for teachers to learn and use technology effectively. In return, technological competence of teachers is mandatory. In other words, schools must "push it," but teachers need to "adopt it." Philip points to a Presidential Election Simulation Game that he used to employ when teaching. Initially, the purchased game, used on an Apple IIe, was designed to simulate the 1984 campaign between Ronald Reagan and Walter Mondale. Reagan won the actual election by an electoral landslide so it was not much fun for those on the Democratic side and the game proved to be a commercial failure for the company. What did Philip do? He modified and restructured the simulation to recreate the 1960 Kennedy/Nixon election instead. He wrote new lesson plans that required his students to learn about the issues and candidates while running their own respective campaigns. In fact, he topped it off by inviting political commentator and journalist, Chris Matthews, to his class to talk about his book on the 1960 election. Whenever Philip played this game, it was common to hear the loud noise of authentic learning by engaged students emanating from his classroom.

## Other Interview Questions

*1. Who is/are your role model(s) from an educational perspective?*

Philip Bigler identifies James Madison and Donald Robertson as outstanding role models.

According to Philip, James Madison was the greatest governmental thinker in the early American republic. He had an intimate understanding of human nature, natural law, and the ultimate purpose of government. Madison, of course, was the fourth President of the United States and is often referred as the "Father of the Constitution," writing over one-third of the *Federalist Papers.*

Donald Robertson was a teacher who ran a small school in Virginia back in the 1760s which the young James Madison attended. Robertson was the educator who introduced many of the ideas of enlightenment to Madison and which helped shape his political philosophy and staunch belief in republicanism. As Madison stated near the end of his life, "All that I have been in my life I owe largely to that man [Robertson]." At James Madison University, Philip established "The Donald Robertson Scholarship in Elementary Education" to recognize current pre-service teachers as well as to celebrate Robertson and the impact that elementary educators have on young people.

*2. When you take a look at teachers, in general, and recognize all the hard work and devotion they put into their jobs, what would you say is the one thing that you think teachers can improve upon so they can become more highly effective?*

Philip believes that teachers must embrace change and be willing to take the risk of failure. Successful teachers continue to change over the time, constantly broadening their perspective and keeping themselves challenged. In his own teaching career, Philip taught 22 different subjects over 23 years in the classroom. From Middle Eastern History to Russian History to Photojournalism, Philip's own intellectual curiosity, and his ability to convey that to others, is what kept his teaching fresh and new. "Teachers need to evolve over their teaching career and should not be the same teacher at the end as they were at the beginning," says Philip. For those teachers who teach the same subject or grade level for an extended period of time, they often become too comfortable which is not necessarily a good thing. Teachers need to embrace change if they desire to be a better teacher.

*3. Are there policies that your school (or past school) has adopted which allow teachers to excel?*

According to Philip, site-based management and recognition of expertise within a school system are two policies that can really help.

Site-based management includes giving the budgetary decision-making to the school. Teachers can guide administrators in terms of purchases for textbooks, classroom resources, and needed technology. This provides a sense of "buy-in" from stakeholders as opposed to feeling powerless from being told what to do.

Recognition of expertise means utilizing outstanding teachers as leaders in their schools, departments, and grade levels. This can manifest itself as team leaders and subject-matter leaders in the school. Faculty workshops, mentor programs, and so forth can be handled this way to capitalize on the existing talent pool.

*4. In order to improve our educational system, what are the shortcomings you notice in schools. What are some of the good things happening? What do you think needs to change?*

Philip notes that there is a general sense that contemporary curricula are being "watered down" to address standards-based testing and agenda-driven pedagogy. While some students may be able to answer high-stakes testing questions, they do not fully understand the underlying concepts. It appears that schools are forcing children into rote memorization rather than embarking on a quest to obtain substantive knowledge. As a humanities teacher, Philip also points to the importance of reading high quality literature. Yet classics such as *Huckleberry Finn* are being used less and less by schools and Philip believes this is a shame. While some vocal critics accuse Twain's novel as being racist, Philip vehemently disagrees. He states, "It is Huck's recognition of Jim as a human being and as a friend rather than a slave that makes Twain's work so brilliant." Philip also believes that students need to be given choices in their reading. That said, it must be high quality literature. For those who choose books based on selective agendas (e.g., green/environment; self-esteem; social justice), they need to be careful. Philip states, "[A teacher's job] is to allow students to explore and help them to think." It is not to push an agenda. Plus, parents should know what students are reading and why.

Philip notes that some of the good things happening in schools include the new crop of young people entering the teaching profession and the opportunities to incorporate technology into learning. Philip notices that the new generation of teachers is highly enthusiastic and idealistic. Moreover, their training tends to be strong due to the enormous and highly qualified preparatory and graduate education programs available. Along the same lines, technology has opened the door and revolutionized the way teachers can reach different types of learners. Nowadays, the sky is the limit and the opportunities to differentiate instruction are immense.

# CHAPTER 22

## Sarah Brown Wessling
National Teacher of the Year (2010)
(English – Grades 10 to 12)

*"We must view young people not as empty bottles to be filled, but as candles to be lit."*
*— Robert Shaffer*

Each year, Sarah Wessling starts the school year with Robert Shaffer's quote. She posts it prominently in her classroom for all students to read. As a teacher, Sarah shares that her primary job is to help students construct their own learning and knowledge. Teaching is not about imparting everything one knows to those whom they teach. Rather, she asserts, "Teaching is meant to help students achieve for themselves." Sarah's educational philosophy proposes that "learning must be learner-centered, it must be constructed, and its power already resides in each person." That is the true essence of good teaching and what it means to be in Sarah's class.

## Background

What is most striking about Sarah Wessling's teaching is that it is all about her students and the belief that she has in each one of them. As she emphasizes, "I see a story in every learner, unique and yearning to be read…I work to see the potential in each one of them that they couldn't see in themselves." Sarah's genuine interest in, and advocacy for, her students create an honest and close student-teacher connection. For this reason, Sarah is a bona fide, student-centered teacher.

Sarah's path to teaching was less of a choice and much more of a realization. Teaching allowed her to combine her varied passions for literature and broadcast journalism with learning psychology and human philosophy. Working as a teacher was the perfect scenario for Sarah. Since 1998, Sarah taught high school English and served in numerous leadership positions at her school. Currently, she splits her time and teaches half-day. During the other half, Sarah serves as Teacher Laureate for Teaching Channel (www.teachingchannel.org), a video showcase – on the Internet and television – of innovative and effective teaching practices in America's schools. Among her other activities, Sarah is heavily involved in professional development practices across the country. She also continues to work with pre-service teachers, often at her alma mater, Iowa State University.

Sarah's body of work in the field of teaching has been recognized by a variety of organizations and institutions. Back in 1998, the Promising Teacher Award was given to Sarah by the Iowa Council of Teachers of English. Since then, she has been recognized as Iowa Governor's Scholastic "Favorite Teacher Award" for 2004 and 2009. Later, Sarah was honored as the 2010 Iowa Teacher of the Year and chosen as the 2010 National Teacher of the Year.

Sarah earned her bachelor's and master's degrees in English from Iowa State University, graduating with distinction. She is a National Board Certified Teacher.

**Teacher Top 5**

1. *Know Your Students*: Sarah "sees the world in stories." So when it comes to her students, there are two stories to discover: who they are as a person; and who they are as a learner. By knowing your students, connections can be made and teachers can understand how best to guide their learning.

As a person, it is important to know who that student is. For instance, how many siblings does he or she have? What does he or she like to do with his or her free time? What is his or her passion? Teachers must have the curiosity and desire to know each student. Every pupil has his or her own story and motivations. It is a teacher's job to know his or her students, and to know them well.

As a learner, it is imperative to understand how each student processes information. In doing so, it guides the teacher. For instance, what kind of feedback does the student respond best? Sarah believes that learning is more about the process of learning, and less about getting the right answer. She stresses, "It's about figuring out how we learn; how we become thinkers."

2. _Be the Lead Learner_: To foster a culture of learning, the teacher must be a learner too. In fact, teachers need to learn alongside students. There should not be a hierarchy whereby the teacher espouses his or her knowledge and simply fills students with information. Sarah declares, "Every person who enters into class is elevated to a level of learner." It is up to the teacher to model this for others to see. Sarah also points out that classrooms differ between tasks-centric versus engagement in learning. As an example, performing a workbook page is doing a task. On the other hand, working through process, promoting a culture where dispositions are valued, and creating opportunities for students to construct their learning are all elements of active learning and real engagement.

3. _Meet Students Where They Are_: "When you know your students' stories, you must meet them where they are," states Sarah. This means working with them at their current skill level, no matter what entry point it happens to be. From there, teachers guide, encourage, and help students develop in their own learning. Sarah calls it, "Taking a walk with students and bringing them with us." In actual practice when a new skill is introduced, Sarah determines each student's current skill level. Some may be ready for the lesson, but others may not. She meets students where they are and differentiates instruction for different learners with varying entry points. In her class, several groups of learners usually exist. That is because Sarah believes in personalizing and individualizing education for each student's need and skill level.

4. _Don't Take Yourself Too Seriously_: As a teacher, it is crucial to have fun and laugh often. Sarah proclaims, "Kids are the greatest truth serum. You can't fake anything in front of them. They know who you

are." For that reason, Sarah recommends, "Be you!" Teachers have the incredible freedom of creating a culture and environment in a classroom. Why not make it fun and genuine? Sarah notes that she truly enjoys her students and their teenage humor. She finds herself laughing all the time, together with her students. It is an honest relationship. Sarah even shares that when she does not think that she has taught a lesson very well, she will reach out to students for their input. This is very important in fostering a culture of authenticity. For Sarah, she keeps it very human in her class.

5. _There's a Great Deal of Humility in Teaching – Be Compassionate_: At the center of teaching is humility. Educators are humble. Teaching is about the students, not the teacher. Sarah establishes, "I am not the stage. I am not the personality of the classroom. It's about them." As a matter of fact, she emphasizes that her job is to make it about them. This means showing compassion and empathy as well as helping students construct their own learning. Along the way, she will grow with them, together. It is not about her. Rather, it is about them. Knowing that, and embracing it for your own teaching, requires humility.

**Other Interview Questions**

_1. Who is/are your role model(s) from an educational perspective?_

According to Sarah, all of the people she has had the opportunity to work with and learn from are her role models. They exist as a collage of people who have been influential in her cumulative education as a teacher and a student. She reflects on certain educators who taught her how to be an effective responder of student work, helped her understand how to create a culture in her environment, and shed light on how to bring laser-like focus in the classroom. Sarah insists,

"What made these people special is that they implemented all five [Sarah's *Teacher Top 5*] of them."

*2. When you take a look at teachers, in general, and recognize all the hard work and devotion they put into their jobs, what would you say is the one thing that you think teachers can improve upon so they can become more highly effective?*

One of the biggest problems with teaching is that teachers are largely isolated. Eventually, the isolation leads to stunted growth. Sarah explains, "We must get out of isolation. Teachers can't go into their classroom and close their doors. It doesn't make them better." In other words, teachers need to collaborate. This can take the form of working with other educators or networking with professional organizations and online communities. Whatever it may be, the purpose is to engage in introspective dialogue about instruction and the craft of teaching. Sarah shares that her involvement at the Teaching Channel is helping to create online communities to get teachers out of isolation. At the website, viewers can watch other teachers teach and pick up techniques. Sarah sees the Teaching Channel and other venues like this as a forum to open up classroom doors so that educators can learn from one another.

*3. Are there policies that your school (or past school) has adopted which allow teachers to excel?*

At her district, Sarah cites that "Late Start Wednesdays" has helped teachers tremendously. Students come to school one hour later, allowing teachers the time to collaborate. Sarah declares, "This is an important time to work with each other [in order] to get better as an educator." Interestingly enough, the idea for "Late Start Wednesdays" came from several teachers at her high school who recognized the importance of teacher collaboration.

Similarly, Sarah believes that a clarity of mission and purpose are critical as schools attempt to progress. In visiting numerous academic institutions as part of her role as National Teacher of the Year, the most outstanding schools retain a concrete knowledge of what they want to accomplish. The goal might be as big as having every student attend college or as simple as something that is project-based. Regardless, an unclouded mission is vital so that all the teachers construe it exactly the same way and adopt it as their own. Thereafter, teachers convey this to students. Ultimately, everyone should be working toward the same goal.

*4. In order to improve our educational system, what are the shortcomings you notice in schools. What are some of the good things happening? What do you think needs to change?*

In keeping with the classroom of learners philosophy, Sarah posits that the hierarchical structure of schools between administrators and teachers need to be flattened. That way, everyone is a learner. School principals should not simply be managers of people, but also leaders of pedagogy, instruction, and curriculum. Administrators who are task managers create a very different culture as compared to instructional guides.

Sarah also advocates creating a system of great teachers. The teaching profession does not necessarily benefit from honoring a single educator in isolation. Instead, the focus should be on systematically elevating all educators so that they can teach more effectively. Sarah identifies the country of Finland as doing a fine job of promoting and developing the teaching profession. She also adds that schools like Adlai Stevenson High School in Lincolnshire, Illinois have done terrific work in professional learning communities. Plus, the Center for Authentic Intellectual Work in Iowa is another institution that provides ongoing teacher professional development to improve the efficacy of all educators.

# CHAPTER 23

## Craig Divis
Vermont State Teacher of the Year (2010)
(Social Studies – Grades 9 to 12)

*"One man's terrorist is another man's freedom fighter."*

*— Anonymous*

As a social studies teacher, Craig believes that one of the biggest challenges is getting high school students to "think about their own thinking." In history, there is never simply one set of facts. As accepted in the popular consciousness, history is written by the victors. Craig knows this to be a truism, especially from an American point-of-view.

In teaching world history, Craig wants students to think for themselves and consider multiple perspectives. "Don't simply accept the news, what your parents, or friends say. Think about who is making these distinctions...as friends or enemies, or in this case, terrorists or freedom fighters," states Craig. As modern day examples, Craig identifies Nelson Mandela and the Dalai Lama. In the past and currently, who is to say that either man is a terrorist or freedom fighter? That is why Craig chose the above quote.

Craig wants students to think critically, understand why multiple viewpoints exist, and recognize that labels can be perpetuated. In his class, Craig's goal is to get students to think about how they view other people and different cultures. In other words, students should be taught how to think as opposed to what to think.

## Background

Craig Divis is a cosmopolitan educator who practices cultural reciprocity with all his heart. As a teacher of world cultures, world history, world geography, senior seminar, and advanced placement European history, Craig has always been fascinated with different cultures and people. It is simply a part of who he is and that is one of the many attributes he brings into his classroom.

Craig teaches, because he says, "I know that's the most important profession in the world." He adds, "Education can open students' minds and that's why I teach. It can show them the world and have them look at the world from a different point of view. It can inspire students to find their passion not just that, but follow that passion, and learn how to be effective in that role."

While teaching history can appear mundane and routine, Craig's teaching style is anything, but dull. Authentic and first-hand, real world experiences are hallmarks of his teaching. In 2011, Craig was recognized as a Fulbright Distinguished Teacher, which allowed him to spend a year in South Africa. There, he worked with teachers and students to learn how the topic of apartheid is taught. This experience, among his many others, is then brought back and applied. It provides a spark to his own classes in Vermont.

In less than a decade of teaching, Craig's accomplishments are plentiful. He was named the 2010 Vermont Teacher of the Year after only six years of teaching. Craig was also given the SMARTer Kids Foundation Teaching Excellence Award and the Vermont Governor's Institute on Asian Cultures Award. Craig serves as the history department chair at his high school and he also teaches Asian Cultures at the University of Vermont.

Craig received his bachelor's in education at Miami University.

**Teacher Top 5**

1. *Have a Passion for Teaching and Content*: While this may seem obvious, it should not be overlooked. Anyone intending to enter the teaching profession really needs to make sure they love to teach young people. Craig asserts, "A successful teacher needs to love teaching to the point where they are willing to do whatever it takes to engage their students and help them learn. Being passionate about teaching is really about motivation and dedication to your job as an educator. It is knowing that teachers have a tremendous responsibility in helping young people learn about the world, about who they

are, and to realize their potential." Teaching is not simply an 8am to 3pm job.

The other aspect is enjoying the content area taught. Craig states, "I have a strong passion for teaching the field of history, and I have seen how this has had a positive impact on students reacting to my energy and excitement in class in a positive manner." Needless to say, enthusiasm and passion are infectious. That is why Craig also believes that it is important for students to see that their teacher enjoys being at school. A teacher cannot expect students to show a love for learning, if he or she does not demonstrate it.

2. _Be Relevant_: For any subject, teachers must make their lessons authentic and relevant for students. "Relevancy is arguably the most important part of each lesson that a teacher must focus on," says Craig. Otherwise, students will not be able to relate to what is being taught. "Teachers need to connect each lesson, activity, assignment, and assessment to their students in order to make the content make more sense, so that it is more applicable. One of the main causes of student apathy and lack of interest in school is that they don't see the connection between class content and their lives and the world today," identifies Craig.

The question, "Why do I have to know this?" is often heard from students. Craig responds by saying, "A successful teacher relates the content to his or her students, and thus personalizes it in order for the students to connect more to it and for the learning to be more lasting." As an example in his history class, students query about the importance and newsworthiness of the civil war in Syria. Craig reaches back to the French, Russian, and American Revolutions to show that civil wars do not simply exist in a static period of time in history. Rather, they evolve and take place in modern times too. Craig also teaches to empower his students to become activists. For instance, the anti-apartheid movement in South Africa was assisted by Americans who put pressure on that country. He shows his students how they can be directly involved.

3. _Have Fun_: Arguably, having fun is one of the most underrated notions about teaching. Many teachers know that a happy climate has an enormous impact on school culture and students' attitudes. That said, not every teacher is cheery. Craig knows, "There are many aspects of teaching that can easily frustrate teachers – new school and state-wide initiatives, constant focus on testing, school boards, teacher unions, etc. – but successful teachers don't get beaten down by these issues and continue to love coming into school every day and working with amazingly talented students."

While an educational setting can be somewhat formal, that should not bar the concept of fun. Craig believes, "Having energy, excitement, and fun in teaching can motivate and engage students, make learning more fun, and decrease behavioral issues in the classroom." Craig suggests bringing humor into the classroom, playing games, and so forth. In his own discipline, history can be quite boring, depending on how it is taught. Hence, it is this challenge – to make it engaging and fun – that can determine a successful teacher.

4. _Put in the Time_: Truth be told, successful teaching takes a formidable amount of time. Teaching does not simply end after dismissal. Even though teachers have personal lives and their own commitments, they need to be ready to go beyond regular work hours. Craig

always makes sure he is one of the first teachers to arrive at his school. Craig states, "Teachers need to put in the time before school and after school to work with students who need extra help." He believes this sends a message to students that he is willing to go out of his way to make sure that they are successful. In return, students will often meet him half-way, putting forth strong effort, knowing that Craig put in the time to work with them.

In terms of improving curricular materials, time is also a factor. Craig says, "Teachers need to work on weekends, breaks, and summers to…[develop original and new assignments, lessons, and assessments] to better reach each and every student in their class." In addition, Craig adds, "Successful teachers don't just focus on their students being successful in their classes, but also outside of school, as well, including in sports, concerts, drama club presentations, and other extracurricular activities and hobbies." By doing so, students will feel that they are supported. That is why making time is essential.

5. _Never Stop Learning_: Teaching is a vastly changing and evolving profession, including new teaching techniques and technology. "Successful teachers never settle for the status quo; they are always looking for better activities and strategies of teaching to improve the learning environment for their students," says Craig. To make sure lifelong learning continues, he suggests, "[A]ttending workshops, conferences, and other professional development opportunities, as well as reading about new trends in education and teaching, to improve…."

As a history teacher, Craig seeks professional development opportunities that take him abroad. Traveling not only provides first-hand experiences that can be brought back into the classroom, but also ignites the spark in his area of content studied. Craig's Fulbright grant, allowing him to travel to South Africa, is a prime example. He learned that technology, like computers and Smart Boards, was not readily available. Therefore, South African educators relied on their intrinsic teaching talents to make teaching fun and compelling. Thoughtful lessons, playful activities, different styles of group work, and oral history research are just some of the ways educators from afar reach their students.

**Other Interview Questions**

*1. Who is/are your role model(s) from an educational perspective?*

There have been a number of role models throughout Craig's education and teaching career.

First, Craig was motivated by his mother, a retired teacher. He says, "[I]t was the passion that she spoke of for teaching and her genuine interest in her students' success that led me to value the profession. I remember being out with my mother at the grocery store or at a restaurant and seeing her former students come up to her with tears in their eyes and hug her, thanking her for everything she did for them. It…showed me the power that a teacher could have in people's lives."

Craig also identifies Mr. Blaha, his high school history teacher. "His passion for history and for taking an interest in his student's lives was amazing. He supported you as a student not only in his classroom, but also outside of it at your sporting events or band concerts. He made you want to work harder in his class, because he actually cared about you as a person, not just as his student," says Craig.

At Miami University, Craig was inspired by Dr. Winkler and Dr. Fuller. Craig claims, "[They] opened my eyes up to how important history is, how exciting it can be, and to the incredible world outside of the borders of the United States....It was these two professors... that I not only became certain that I wanted to teach, but I became certain how I wanted to teach."

Lastly, Craig recognizes his students. He states, "[They] have taught me more about teaching and about learning than any course or textbook could ever do....It is not about a grade on a test or getting an essay in on time. It is about helping students find their passion and encouraging them to follow it. It is about motivating students to be global citizens. I now get more satisfaction out of a student who is excited to come in and discuss a news story with me or who wants to apply for a study abroad program than one who gets an A+ on a research paper."

*2. When you take a look at teachers, in general, and recognize all the hard work and devotion they put into their jobs, what would you say is the one thing that you think teachers can improve upon so they can become more highly effective?*

Craig is aware of the globalization occurring all around us. Therefore, he believes that it needs to be taught and understood. He declares, "One thing teachers can do to be more effective is to be more globally-based in their approach in terms of content. The world that today's students will be entering when they graduate is one that is becoming more and more interconnected. In order to prepare students to be successful, education needs to adapt and to provide the tools and opportunity to succeed in this global landscape. Through globalization, nations and companies have broken down borders and the barriers of language and culture. Now, education, too, needs to come out of its slumber and be prepared to make the necessary changes."

When asked how to execute this global strategy, Craig states, "The solution is to internationalize education in all aspects. For example, our course offerings need to be more globally-based and realistic, with mandatory courses such as World Cultures and more relevant foreign language offerings such as Mandarin Chinese and Arabic. Just as how math and science were stressed during the Cold War's arms race in the 1950s, we now need to change our focus to include a globalized curriculum. In addition to new course offerings and curriculum, this emphasis on global education needs to begin as early as the elementary level in order to give students the best chance at success in today's competitive world." Furthermore, he adds, "This new global education cannot take place solely in the traditional classroom, as it is not relevant to today's student. We need to take advantage of offering more Web-based courses and more study abroad and student-teacher exchange programs. The traditional classroom environment does not stand a chance compared to these international cultural experiences."

*3. Are there policies that your school (or past school) has adopted which allow teachers to excel?*

Craig's school district provides teachers with quite a bit of latitude, regarding how they teach and meet state standards. For this, he considers himself lucky. Craig states, "My school supports teachers by giving them the freedom to teach how they want, and to experiment with new methodologies and strategies. This is vitally important as I feel that I am not constrained to teach one particular way regardless of how my students want to learn or their learning styles. This freedom not only shows respect for me as a professional, but also allows me the ability to try new things with my teaching."

A good example is Craig's use of guided inquiry. In this case, Craig says, "[S]tudents decide what topic we will be learning about during a unit and they work much more independently throughout the unit on their project. The key is that they decide what they want to be learning about and how they do it." This teaching technique is a skills-based approach as opposed to an approach which relies on just memorizing facts.

*4. In order to improve our educational system, what are the shortcomings you notice in schools. What are some of the good things happening? What do you think needs to change?*

Craig says, "There are many issues in public education today that I feel are important in being able to better reach the 21st century student, ranging from technology in the classroom, international or globally-based education, participatory education, and the importance and necessity of social studies. Today's students require a very different education than in the past, as they need to be prepared to succeed in an ever-evolving global community, and to be able to ready them for the challenges they will experience. Education needs to have a different focus, both in the content as well as in the teaching style."

As far as shortcomings, Craig identifies a myriad of opportunities for improvement. He states, "Shortcomings in education include an overemphasis on standardized testing, a lack of emphasis on the importance of the content and skills that the social studies teach, too much emphasis on state mandates that leave schools simply passing students along to meet state graduation levels, unmotivated teachers who are not willing to change with the times, and teachers unions who do not have the students as their first priority."

In addressing the good things happening, Craig shares, "Teachers are finding amazing ways to integrate technology into the classroom and of connecting their students to other students around the world." Software and Internet tools like Google Sketch Up are readily used by students. For instance, students can design a museum for a European history class. Students can also utilize technology to create public service announcements in print, audio, and visual formats. Thereafter, they can publish on Youtube and a variety of other platforms. Craig declares, "It is a great time to be a teacher and very exciting to see so many amazing and innovative new ways of teaching that teachers are coming into the classroom."

# CHAPTER 24

## James Smith

New Mexico State Teacher of the Year (2003)
(History – Grades 10 to 12)

*"Leap and the net will appear."*
— *John Burroughs*

Taking chances can mean different things to different people. Some people believe in something so passionately that deep down in their heart they know that someone or something will appear and embrace what they are reaching for, rather than allowing them to fall to the ground. That is the general meaning of American author, John Burroughs' quote.

In Jim Smith's office, Burroughs' words hang prominently on the wall. Jim states, "It's how I did and do things as a writer and teacher. You just sort of have to take chances. You have to have the audacity to try things and get out there and do it. Trust that there will be something there to catch you." This has been Jim's philosophy since the very start of his teaching career and it remains a tenet in his current profession as a writer. It is about taking chances and trusting yourself.

In the classroom, Jim promoted this philosophy to his students. Jim says, "It's the idea that you can't stay in your safe zone, your comfort zone, all of the time....You have to try to get out there in the world and try to make something of yourself...and trust that something will be there to catch you. Trust that you don't have to do it all alone." In order for students to dive into their greatness, they have to go head first. No fear, all commitment.

**Background**

The year 1974 was an amalgamation of a number of important events. The highest profile news was Richard Nixon becoming the only sitting United States President to resign from office. With such unsettling news, a grand push to improve the moral character and betterment of society took hold. Jim Smith was part of that generation to restore the integrity of the country. As a high school senior, the thought of becoming a teacher entered his mind. Jim states, "It wasn't about making money. It wasn't about being famous. It was about doing something to make your world a little bit better." For that reason, Jim began his teaching career as a history educator. Eventually, it would lead to over 30 years in the public school system.

One of the single most distinguishing aspects of Jim is his infinite passion for history. He declares, "Whether I am providing high school students a few tips on how to write an argumentative essay or helping adults understand a Beethoven symphony, I am always, in some way, trying to promote the study of history. I believe that history, when taught well, can be a humanizing subject that helps people put their lives in context and see something bigger than themselves. I am motivated by the hope that when more people have a better sense of history our world might become just a little more rational and humane." This guiding thesis allowed Jim to become an exceptional teacher recognized by numerous organizations and institutions. Some of his awards include, but are not limited to, the 2003 New Mexico Teacher of the Year, Finalist for the National Teachers Hall of Fame, and the Gilder-Lehrman Institute of American History United States History Teacher of the Year. In the past, Jim was a recipient of the James Madison Fellowship, the Christa McAuliffe Fellowship, and a two-time recipient of the William Robertson Coe Fellowship.

While Jim has retired from daily classroom teaching, he remains active as an education consultant, writer, publisher, and part-time teacher. Jim is also an author of several books, including an American history textbook entitled *Ideas That Shape a Nation* and *Catherine's Son: The Story of a Boy Who Became an Outlaw*.

Jim holds a bachelor's degree in education focused on history and music, as well as two master's degrees in history and government from New Mexico State University.

**Teacher Top 5**

1. *Never Enter a Classroom Unprepared*: It is a real challenge to manage students of any age. A variety of studies suggest that roughly 33% of all new teachers leave the profession after three years, and 46% quit within five years.[2] Jim says, "For young teachers, classroom management is one of the biggest problems…my recommendation is to prepare really good lessons, know what you are doing, and enter a classroom overprepared. That will allow you to survive the profession." Built into this logic is that teachers need to be organized and think things deeply through. Jim points out, "Students don't want you to waste their time….Students have a good sense that they know the teachers who know what they're doing." All of this preparedness benefits not only the students, but also the teacher. All teachers know when their classroom is running efficiently and effectively. By adopting this first principle, a career in teaching has less chance of premature abdication.

2. *Find a Way to Motivate and Inspire Students*: Jim believes that this is the crux of teaching. He shares, "I believe that's 90% of teaching. If the students are motivated, you can do a lot with them…I believe that's where all good teaching begins." He adds, "If you have 50 teachers, there are 50 ways of being a good teacher. But almost all of these would start with the same thing in motivating and inspiring your students." Jim recommends employing a teaching style that fits your own personality. Teachers must be authentic. Students know a fake when they see one. Jim also states, "You have to be the author of your own words. You can't do it the way Jim Smith did it, because you don't have the same personality."

As a teacher, Jim's technique mirrored his soft-spoken demeanor. He attests, "My motivation came from them sensing that I was on their side. I was not out to get them. I was there to help. I motivated through good content, and made history so interesting that when they left the classroom, they were still talking about it." That comes from a strong depth of knowledge, riveting presentation of material, stimulating readings, fun activities, and simulation games.

3. _Never Quit Learning and Growing as a Teacher_: "Teaching is the sort of job you never get right," confesses Jim. Even after 30 years of experience, he would occasionally find himself making mistakes of a rank amateur. Much of teaching depends on the students. Jim declares, "First period, I may be on top of the world. Second period, I may be in the pits of hell." That is why it is so important to continue learning and growing as a teacher. Seasoned educators can learn from new graduates and vice versa. In the building, teachers need to talk, share ideas, and collaborate. At the district level, professional learning communities need to be instituted so that teachers get together and discuss the best ways to teach students. Professional development should be made available over the entire career of teachers. Most of all, Jim encourages teachers to read about what is happening in their profession and content-matter. For today's teacher, Jim says, "You have to have a huge bag of tricks, learn new strategies, and stay up with what's happening with issues in education."

4. _Bring a Sense of Playfulness into the Classroom_: Jim calls this the heart and joy of learning. Teachers need to bring a good sense of humor into the classroom. Over time, this has become challenging due to the emphasis of standardized testing and strict compliance with standards. Still, Jim urges new teachers to make learning fun.

Learning, if done effectively, should be synonymous with fun. He states, "For the new teacher, it is okay to be playful. Have fun and enjoy it."

In his class, historical simulation games were a way of bringing out the best in his students. A prime example was the re-creation of the 1850s during the Civil War. Students played North and South senators. Jim says, "Allow them to ham it up (with accents). Laugh along with them. Laugh at yourself and bring in fun little anecdotes."

5. _Have Faith in Youth_: "You can't last in the profession unless you believe in youth. They are the future," declares Jim. Students are the next generation of leaders and belief in their potential is tantamount. The current state of education, however, is perplexing. Jim points out, "The standards and centralization of curriculum have made it difficult and taken out the artistry in teaching...[it] doesn't allow for creativity and innovation." Since all learners are different and each student's education should be individualized, what's happening in education – a one-size-fits-all approach – appears to be subverting what is sometimes best for students. In this case, Jim states, "I see no way else but to connect with kids and inspire them...to leave the script. I don't know how reading a script and finding a lesson inspires anybody."

## Other Interview Questions

_1. Who is/are your role model(s) from an educational perspective?_

In remembering his educators as great role models, Jim explains that it is not just how he or she teaches or what was taught, but rather who the teacher was as a person. Jim comments, "You always remember somebody, how he or she made you feel."

Jim singles out his late high school teacher, Jack Hall, as his outstanding role model. "I learned from Mr. Hall that a knowledge of history led to an understanding of universal truths about human nature and helped people gain wisdom through an understanding of human behavior. To Mr. Hall, history was an academic discipline that helped people define themselves as individuals and as members of a community." Jim continues, "Jack Hall was just a good human being…honest, decent, intellectually curious, cared about kids, and dedicated to teaching."

*2. When you take a look at teachers, in general, and recognize all the hard work and devotion they put into their jobs, what would you say is the one thing that you think teachers can improve upon so they can become more highly effective?*

As touched upon previously, Jim suggests, "Find a way to be creative and innovative with students. Bring a sense of playfulness and good humor into the classroom." By accomplishing that, students will meet and exceed their full potential. Lastly, teachers should not allow high-stakes testing and rigid standards constrict their teaching. There is always a way for teachers to adjust their teaching so that they can reach their students.

*3. Are there policies that your school (or past school) has adopted which allow teachers to excel?*

"The best schools, it seems to me, are the ones where administrators create an atmosphere where good teachers can thrive, giving teachers some autonomy and trusting them as professionals to do what's best for students," says Jim.

In his own experience, Jim praises the leadership of retired principal Robert Ogas of Mayfield High School in Las Cruces, New Mexico. Jim remembers Principal Ogas for his effective hiring practices, ability to manage difficult issues, and autonomy he gave to teachers. In the core subjects and almost all of the elective areas, master teachers were in the classroom. Principal Ogas also acted as a steadfast gatekeeper, handling central office and parental problems. He would take care of these issues so that teachers could focus on what they do best: teach. Teachers were encouraged to be creative and given autonomy to do so. Principal Ogas was also a strong, consistent, and fair disciplinarian who had high expectations and delivered consequences. Jim concludes, "He created an atmosphere and culture of excellence. New teachers who came, felt it and wanted to be good…he had one of the best math and English teachers, the top music department in the state, and championship sports teams…this wasn't a school district where you think you'd have all those things."

*4. In order to improve our educational system, what are the shortcomings you notice in schools. What are some of the good things happening? What do you think needs to change?*

First and foremost, Jim states, "The ubiquitous testing that is accompanied by the standardization and centralization of curriculum have taken the artistry out of teaching. I would give teachers greater autonomy, trust them as professionals, and encourage them to be creative and innovative in the delivery of instruction."

Jim does not believe that the constant measuring of teacher and student performance is the key to educational success. He believes that teaching is an art form and there is no one right way to do it. Jim states, "It's like great art. You've got to inspire people. You know great art when you see it. That's how you know great teaching."

Jim points out that over time the nature of the teaching profession has changed. Jim believes that teachers are not "the" content specialist for whom everybody goes. He says, "The teacher used to be like Google. Now, you can look things up. Kids have instant information in their pocket." That said, teachers are still needed to inspire, lead, guide, and develop thinking skills. Jim comments, "Something technology can't do is to teach you to think. Teach analytical thinking and give opportunities to think creatively. Those things can only happen in a classroom where you're interacting with other students and teachers."

# CHAPTER 25

## John Mick Sharkey
Idaho State Teacher of the Year (2006)
(Biological Sciences – Grades 10 to 12)

*"Hell, there are no rules here; we're trying to build something."*
— *Thomas Edison*

After shortly joining Thomas Edison's staff at his Menlo Park Laboratory, Martin André Rosanoff, a Paris-trained chemist, asked Mr. Edison what the rules and regulations were at his laboratory. In response, Thomas Edison spat on the floor and said, "Hell, there are no rules here; we're trying to build something."

This direct and no-nonsense Edison quote is Mick Sharkey's favorite. He states, "In education, we use a lot of labels on kids. The labels have rules [e.g., students with an Individualized Education Program (IEP)]....It can be helpful, but sometimes it's not very helpful. It's harmful." Before an IEP can be implemented, schools must conduct a full evaluation of a student's disability. Thereafter, a variety of stakeholders – educational specialists, teachers, administrators, and parents – come together to determine what, if any, special education services are required.

What does Mick think of all of this? He comments, "I've found that if you can get a kid to believe that he or she can do it, the label falls away." In fact, if there is too much emphasis on what a student cannot do, Mick shares, "[T]he kids believe in their own labels." That is why Thomas Edison's quote resonates. In his classroom, there are no rules. There are no labels. "We're trying to get something done here," quips Mick.

**Background**

As a young person, Mick Sharkey went through the parochial school system in Butte, Montana, but claims that he was a "C" student who simply did not apply himself. Mick explains, "In high school, Cs were good enough...I coasted through without ever working." Unfortunately, when Mick went to college, he was not prepared. Subsequently, he dropped out. When he self-reflects, Mick states, "I [wish I could] go back and grab that young man and shake him around in his shirt and explain things to him. He'd have been better off."

That is what Mick does for his students now. He is highly vigilant about every child, making certain that no pupil falls through the cracks. At his school, teams have been specifically set up to make contact with any student who is struggling academically. Mick says,

"I impress on students that Ds and Fs are not acceptable…[and] Cs are not good enough." He adds, "I came through the system as a mediocre product, and I don't want them to come through the system as a mediocre product."

Fast-forward beyond his teen years, Mick Sharkey resembles nothing mediocre, and is quite exceptional. Before teaching, Mick ascended the retail grocery business, starting out as a box boy and ending up in management. Thereafter, he went back and attained a bachelor's degree in biology at 34 years of age. Influenced by his wife who was an educator, Mick turned to teaching, becoming a highly recognized and sought after teacher. In fact, Mick was named the 2006 Idaho State Teacher of the Year. Among his many awards, Mick was also chosen as the 2007 Envitrogen/Biogen Biotechnology National Teacher of the Year Runner Up and was presented the 2006 Thomas O. Bell Excellence in Education Award.

Mick holds a bachelor's of science degree in biology and minor in chemistry from Boise State University. He is known for his cutting edge biology instruction and application of state-of-the art science equipment to teach students.

**Teacher Top 5**

1. _Grade Only What Counts, Perform Student Self-Assessment, and Provide Meaningful, Timely Feedback_: Having pinpoint focus on what truly counts is essential. In Mick's gradebook, the only grades that exist are for tests from "learning targets," derived from state and national standards. Mick declares, "The only thing in my gradebook is what's important, whether or not they know the material." While students are given homework and quizzes, none of them are entered.

That said, immediate and meaningful feedback is always provided for everything turned in and reviewed. "I demand a lot from them, and they have a right to demand a lot from me. So, I try to make the turnaround immediate like the next day or same day," acknowledges Mick.

Along the same lines, students self-assess regularly. After each question on a quiz, there is an "A" (fill in learning targets adequately) and "K" (I know it) column for each student to check off. When everyone is finished, students check their answers on a posted answer key. Thereafter, Mick takes surveys and reviews questions that were missed. "If everyone misses a specific question, it's not a student issue, it's a curriculum delivery problem," states Mick. Therefore, Mick will go back and reteach.

2. _Demonstrate the Relevance in Your Curriculum and Raise the Bar High_: A long time ago, students had to learn what was taught simply because that is what their teacher instructed. Nowadays, students want to know "Why?" Mick says, "When students see the relevance, it's a lot easier to teach them." For instance, when Mick covers the topic of cells in his biology class, real-life connections are essential to developing comprehension. To students, he explains, "Medicine doesn't just focus on the health of the body, but the health of cells. Any symptom or ache you have occurs because cells are not performing at their optimum." By distilling concepts to their rudimentary level, student understanding increases and buy-in results.

In teaching, Mick makes certain that his curriculum not only meets Idaho standards, but exceeds them, pulling from national and other state standards. He has high expectations of his students. This often means doing whatever it takes as a teacher to elevate his students' learning. Mick asserts, "I make myself totally accessible…at lunch, before school, after school, going in on Saturdays, talking with parents, calling home." He adds, "For good teachers, it's not a job. It's their life."

3. _Get Students to Believe They Can Do It_: This mantra is arguably Mick's most important teaching strategy. When teachers convince students that they can be successful, it becomes a self-fulfilling prophecy. To accomplish this, Mick is open and honest with his students. He talks, all the time, about how he believes in them and how he dislikes the labeling established in education. Mick states, "It's telling them over and over again that they can do it. It's an attitude through the entire curriculum and class. And, [when they succeed] you reward the heck out of them."

A prime example was a student who was known for her ornery attitude and tendency to shut down if she did not like the teacher or subject. Mick took her as his student aide and made her his special project. Mick developed a student-teacher relationship of mutual respect, teaching her patience, hard work, and acceptance of others. Over time, she turned her poor academic grades to As, Bs, and Cs. Mick admits, "I talked to her all the time and got her believing. She is an amazing young lady."

4. _Operate with the Mindset that Students Come First_: "All decisions have to be based on what's best for the kids," says Mick. "Students come first, teachers second, and everything else somewhere down the line." This educational philosophy breeds good schools, and even better students. However, it begins with good teachers who are

effective, willing to sacrifice, and see teaching as their life as opposed to a job.

A case in point was the desire to enhance the rigor of Mick's school. Instead of simply meeting the state's graduation requirements of three years of math and two years of science to graduate from high school, Mick's school proposed four years of math and three years of science. In order to accomplish this, teachers had to cut their prep times in half and teach an additional class. While it created high demands on the teachers, everyone agreed, because they understood the importance of preparing students for college.

5. *Help your Principal When You Can, They Need It!*: Over his teaching career, Mick has had seven different principals and seen them come and go. Some were lackluster, but Mick states, "When you [find yourself with] a great principal, help them out. They need your help." The job of administrator is demanding, and teachers can often lend a hand. This also includes speaking truthfully about administrative proposals and rules.

After attending a conference, one of his principals came away with an idea of having every teacher fill-out a daily decision-making sheet. Throughout the academic day, teachers were asked to mark on a sheet each time they made certain types of decisions. When it was presented to Mick, he said, "I'll be honest with you. I'm not going to do this." While this disappointed his principal, Mick prides himself as a straight-shooter who has no issue speaking truth to power. In the end, the principal reconvened with Mick and they talked. What the principal learned via Mick was that this proposal diminished the teacher and treated each like he or she was not a professional. Hence, it would create ill-will among faculty and have negative repercussions. Candid and insightful conversations, like these, help principals who may not have a pulse on matters.

## Other Interview Questions

*1. Who is/are your role-model(s) from an educational perspective?*

As a student teacher, Mick was fortunate to be trained under Paul Broomhall, a former Idaho State Teacher of the Year. Mick states, "His common sense approach, as well as usable and meaningful advice, stood well with me when things got dicey. When he was no longer available, I often asked myself what he would do in tough situations." This common sense approach to education is a philosophy Mick has adopted. Frequently, Mick ignores the labels put on children and uses what works best for his kids. He says, "If you boil the fat off [all the newfangled ideas], good teachers use good common sense and approaches that are known to work."

*2. When you take a look at teachers, in general, and recognize all the hard work and devotion they put into their jobs, what would you say is the one thing that you think teachers can improve upon so they can become more highly effective?*

Developing appropriate and accurate assessments that truly measure what students know is extremely important. At his school, Mick serves not only as a teacher, but also as the information technology director, responsible for helping teachers build their grade book. Mick comments, "I see too many different forms of assessment that are not useful or do not work well. Not much is done in terms of training teachers how to build good assessment tools." Some teachers give students extra credit for coming to class on time, having their parents show up at parent-teacher conferences, or not using their allotted bathroom passes during class. While teachers should be given flexibility, artificial inflation of grades through incentives for extra credit is not meaningful for students, parents, or the school.

*3. Are there policies that your school (or past school) has adopted which allow teachers to excel?*

At the school building level, Mick finds his leadership – school board and superintendent – and community exceptionally supportive. That said, it has been enormously difficult for teachers to further their learning due to the lack of funding on a state and federal level. Mick declares, "Teachers need time to go to conferences and learn…the state has cut funding and federal funding has been reduced….There is no money for textbooks let alone programs that promote excellence and positive feedback." For that reason, professional development is nearly nonexistent for teachers. This is an enormous shortcoming. Similarly, Mick shares, "Idaho ranks 50th in the nation for spending per capita per student." In fact, 2012 represents the second year in a row that Idaho has ranked last in the nation in spending. It is harder to excel when facing these all too common limitations.

*4. In order to improve our educational system, what are the shortcomings you notice in schools. What are some of the good things happening? What do you think needs to change?*

Mick explains, "I am lucky. I come from an excellent school system. We are involved daily with the process of becoming better. We honestly look at what we are doing; make hard and sometimes unpopular decisions on how to improve; and always keep our students' best interest at the forefront." He continues, "We have built an atmosphere that promotes and supports good teachers, while at the same time makes poor teachers feel uncomfortable, and sometimes even unwanted." Initially, poor performing teachers are supported by faculty. However, if their performance is due to their lack of commitment and unwillingness to do their job, much of the faculty at Mick's school will "turn a cold shoulder."

In terms of students seeking to further their education beyond high school, Mick's school and community are tremendously supportive. Mick shares that the school's counselor was a wizard in identifying scholarships available for students. In addition, community scholarships exist. The Bruce Mitchell Foundation, for example, was started by a local businessman whose life was turned around by local high school teachers. The Foundation commits $3,000 to $5,000 per year for every graduating student who desires to continue his or her education, so long as the graduate retains a 3.0 GPA and one letter of recommendation from a faculty member. The local community also started the Save Our Student Fund that raises money for kids going onto vocational school or college. Mick shares, "Our community is extremely supportive of our efforts and we have great kids....This is a great place to teach. It really is."

# CONCLUSION

## What are the Common Themes and Take-Aways?

In an article in *Spirit* magazine about America's Best Teachers 2011, the headline reads, "You need one person to believe in you in your entire life, just one. Often, that one person is a teacher." This quote is absolutely, unequivocally true. It strikes at the heart of what teaching is, and the power of a meaningful student-teacher relationship. Teachers have always played a prominent role in students' lives. Through guidance, mentoring, and coaching, teachers have the unique opportunity to affect change and to produce positive outcomes. In fact, when you think about all of the professions that can truly serve the greater good and impact the next generation, teaching is at the top of the list.

Among the outstanding teachers interviewed in *Teacher Top 5*, common themes for successful teaching emerge. While much of the content is derived from the teachers profiled, the perspectives of other educators are also included, such as Jim Munger (former President of the Board of Directors of the California Association of Independent Schools) and Reveta Bowers (Head of School at the Center of Early Education). It is important to note that certain teaching strategies may be called different names by different educators, but their general educational philosophies remain the same. What works for one teacher, however, may not work for another. That is because all educators know that teaching is much more of an art than a science.

With that in mind, the following represents the most popular *Teacher Top 5* teaching strategies employed by the numerous educators interviewed.

1. Always Strive to Improve
2. Develop Strong Relationships
3. Make Learning Relevant
4. Be Prepared with Purpose
5. Embrace Passion in Everything You Do

## 1. Always Strive to Improve

Seeking ways to improve is often easier said than done. It takes considerable humility, self-initiative, intellectual curiosity, and a little bit of perfectionism. Perhaps the first place to start is to recognize that everything and anything can always be done better. Bob Feurer, the 2011 Nebraska State Teacher of the Year, calls it "*Kaizen*," also known as continuous improvement. With that mantra, the status quo is not good enough and complacency – in teaching the same way, year after year – is unacceptable. Many of the educators interviewed encourage a commitment to lifelong learning. Burt Saxon, the 2005 Connecticut State Teacher of the Year, says that it is imperative to "make a lifelong commitment to becoming a better teacher." This means many things and includes performing regular self-reflection, developing content mastery, and pursuing professional development opportunities that are truly meaningful and taught specifically by classroom educators.

Many of the best teachers do not wait for administrator suggestions during observations or reviews to improve their overall teaching. Effective educators self-initiate on a daily basis to find ways to get better, especially when they already know their strengths and weaknesses. As an example, a number of interviewed teachers admitted their lack of in-depth knowledge of technology. They also realized that technology has evolved considerably. Needless to say, a generation gap in the use of technology exists between teacher and students. While the admissions may appear detrimental on the surface, these same educators showed a resiliency to seek out technically-savvy counterparts whom they could learn from or classes that they could attend. This openness to learn and collaborate is consistent with all interviewees. Kathleen Brody, literacy specialist and professor, put it, "Surround yourself with exemplary people and find two to three high quality teachers who are willing to share and tap them as a resource. Bouncing ideas off of another educator who you respect allows for greater clarity and understanding."

In the quest to improve as an educator and enhance student learning, many interviewees shared that taking risks are essential. It is one of the qualities that differentiate teachers who desire to improve for the sake of their students versus those who are complacent. National Teacher Hall of Fame inductee, Ron Poplau, consistently takes measured risks in order to expose his students to multiple perspectives, no matter how controversial the issue. As a community service educator, Ron invited both the Ku Klux Klan and Black Muslims to speak to students on the same day. Ron acknowledged that both are hate groups with diametrically opposite viewpoints. With that said, it offered students a panorama of real-life biases that exist in the world.

Attempting to execute something that a teacher has not tried before, but wholeheartedly believes in, is a sign of growth and confidence. Myrra Lee, the 1977 National Teacher of the Year, was a pioneer in shedding light on taboo topics such as suicide and sexual abuse in her women's studies class. Myrra's educational philosophy, to involve young people in their own education, allowed a certain level of openness and risk-taking in her classroom. It was not only a nurturing, safe, and inclusive environment where everyone felt comfortable participating, but student thoughts, perspectives, and experiences were also respected. This ultimately led to deep conversations and a higher level of understanding.

Additional risk-taking advice echoed by the teachers interviewed includes, but is not limited to: "Don't be afraid to make mistakes" and "Every failure is an opportunity for success." Since the world is not stagnant, teachers must constantly evolve. For that reason, taking risks in a deliberative fashion is simply part of striving to get better.

## 2. Develop Strong Relationships

Everyone knows the difference between a close friend and a stranger. A good friend can be a confidante who is trusted instinctively. He or she always has your best intentions in mind. Smiles are genuine. You believe in what he or she says. Most of all, a friend cares, and the recipient reciprocates. A stranger, on the other hand, is just about the exact opposite of a close friend. Who is this person? Does he or she even know who I am? Conversations are usually stilted. Can you trust what he or she says? The differences are stark. As a result, teachers must and need to develop a strong relationship with their students and parents/guardians, just like a close friend. Without it, they are simply strangers, delivering instruction in class.

Many of the interviewees believe that relationship-building must exist well before any constituent arrives in the classroom. Intangible relationships begin by developing an outstanding reputation as a teacher at school. If a teacher possesses a phenomenal reputation, he or she has already established a certain amount of credibility, trust, and respect. Teachers need to remember that students and adults talk, outside of the classroom, about who is a good teacher and who they would like to have as a teacher. Prior to the beginning of school, many teachers share they do something to connect with students, parents, and guardians. This can be a letter, phone call, an invitation to meet, or another creative idea. Jason Fulmer, the 2004 South Carolina State Teacher of the Year, states, "I would…send postcards to families over the summer that describe a little bit about what third grade would be like. At pre-open house, I'd have a science fair board with a picture of me on it from when I was in third grade so the kids can see that I was just like them, and a part of the same learning process." This sets the stage so that no person is a stranger when he or she enters class on the first day of school.

Building strong relationships is not only about creating trust and caring. It is also about feelings. How do students feel about their teacher? For almost every interviewed educator, it was commonplace to hear, "Years later, students don't remember what you taught them; however, they remember how you made them feel." This comment was so consistent across the board that it cannot be underscored enough. Students are fantastic listeners and observers. They understand body language, can discern sincerity, and know whether a teacher is up to snuff. Oftentimes, interviewees talked about the little things that students would remember, even though it might have been something minor to the teacher. Joe Masiello, the 2011 Delaware State Teacher of the Year, recounted an experience where he complimented a modest student in his creative writing class who was having difficulty in school and at home. Six months later, this same student confided to Joe that his single compliment turned around her entire perspective about school and how she felt. For such morale-boosting effect, Joe declares, "It cost me nothing, but it gave her so very much." Educators, therefore, must remember that they have enormous influence and power in the classroom. Every word spoken and interaction partaken needs to be deliberate and well thought out. This applies to students not only in a teacher's classroom, but also to any other child whom teachers encounter throughout the day. After all, teaching is a humanistic occupation where the learner is not simply a mechanical robot without feelings.

Relationship-building, knowing your students well, and student empowerment are all interrelated. Many interviewees talked about the importance of knowing their students as people. If teachers possess a deep understanding of their students, they will know exactly how to motivate and guide them. Angela Wilson, a 2012 National Teacher of the Year Finalist, states, "The only way to know each child is to develop relationships. Some people see this as 'fluff'…but without relationships, life-long learning cannot take place….Relationships and connections are the single most valuable use of a teacher's time." Even the most disinterested student can be compelled to become engaged. Even the most dependent student can be taught how to take ownership of his or her own learning. The important aspect is to develop a strong relationship and find ways to empower students on a daily basis. Through mutual trust and plenty of opportunities to demonstrate growth, students can develop maturity which almost always leads to empowerment. As Angela states about students with whom a solid rapport is built, "They'll exceed your expectations of them every single time."

As a final point, establishing rapport with parents and guardians is just as important as with students. Some interviewees call it, "Investing in parent and guardian interaction." Wilma Ortiz, the 2011 Massachusetts State Teacher of the Year, believes that having parents feel like they are a part of their child's learning process is vital. Wilma asserts, "It's so important in the equation of academic success…[teachers need to] promote, encourage, and provide opportunities for parent and guardian involvement and engagement." In many instances, parents and guardians can be a teacher's biggest advocate in reaching their own children and smoothing over other adults who may not be familiar with the teacher. The important part is to maintain communication routinely throughout the year. Good news as well as bad news should always be shared. All too often, parents and guardians only hear from the teacher when something goes awry. Why not make it a point to share the good news too? That, arguably, develops rapport even quicker and stronger. It shows that the teacher sees and looks for the good in children. Plus, when and if there is bad news to follow, parents will take this news better, because they know that the teacher had been looking for positive attributes first. With both children and adults, developing strong relationships is imperative and teachers must remember, "Don't be a stranger."

### 3. Make Learning Relevant

The esteemed educator John Dewey stated, "Education is not preparation for life; education is life itself." This philosophy touches upon all aspects of making learning relevant for students. Interviewed teachers call it, "Keep it real," "Set the context," "Provide culturally relevant curriculum," "Get outside the classroom," and "Wrap the student around the curriculum." No matter the terminology, it all means teaching in a way that truly resonates with students based on their backgrounds, experiences, and what they see in their everyday world. It is not teaching curriculum in isolation with little or no connections to what students know. Rather, it is authentic and leads to inquiry.

When new material is introduced, many interviewees often remarked that students asked, "Why do I need to know this?" Les Nicholas, NEA Member Benefits Award winner, says, "The key to teaching creatively and achieving academic results is by combining relevance with rigor. When students recognize they will actually use the material they are studying, motivation becomes self-directed." That is why Les built a radio and television studio for his journalism class. He ran it like a professional newsgathering organization where students felt like they were going to work as opposed to coming to class. Interestingly enough, the prime cause of student apathy and lack of interest in schools is that many students do not see how class content relates to their daily lives. If teachers can establish the context for what students are learning, then they will understand why it is important to become versed in such topics. One way to connect subject-matter studied to the real world is to distill concepts to its most rudimentary level. Simplify and bring in every day examples and analogies. Another way is to make connections on a micro-level, and then slowly move to a macro-perspective. Either way, all interviewed teachers suggest taking ample time to explain. If in-class time is not enough, always be available before and after school, as well as lunch, to answer questions and clarify concepts taught.

Culturally relevant teaching is another form of pedagogy important to making learning relevant. It asks teachers to take into consideration the ethnic diversity of their student population when instructing. All students cannot be taught the same way. Rhode Island 2008 State Teacher of the Year, George Goodfellow, points out that students from Massachusetts construe and internalize subject-matter differently compared to children from a Navaho Indian community in the Southwest. That means teachers must custom-tailor their lessons, activities, assignments, and assessments to fit the students they are teaching. This varies from state-to-state, class-to-class, and student-to-student. Teaching must be student-centered, not one-size-fits-all.

Finally, if a picture is worth a thousand words, what is a real-life experience worth? Many interviewees believe the value is priceless and there is absolutely no substitute. That is why getting outside of the four walls of a classroom is crucial. Whether it is expeditionary learning, working on an arboretum that serves as an outdoor classroom, going on memorable field trips, or listening to live guest speakers, authenticity must be the goal. Teachers should also take advantage of making cross-curricular and cross-subject connections. Math, science, language arts, social science, and music can be taught interconnectedly, one-way or another.

## 4. Be Prepared with Purpose

While teacher preparedness may seem obvious, a study by the National Commission on Teaching and America's Future reveals that approximately 33% of all new teachers leave teaching after three years. In fact, 46% of new teachers exit the occupation permanently within five years. There are many reasons for departure, but solid preparation, or better yet overpreparation, will make teaching much more enjoyable and improve a teacher's longevity in the profession. Jim Smith, the 2003 New Mexico State Teacher of the Year, shares, "For young teachers, classroom management is one of the biggest problems... my recommendation is to prepare really good lessons, know what you are doing, and enter a classroom overprepared. That will allow you to survive the profession." Moreover, it will help both the teacher and the students. Some say, as a matter of fact, that preparedness is the single most important secret for teacher happiness. Otherwise, the daily grind of delivering instruction, managing students, and taking care a whole host of demands will eventually lead to burn-out, ending in premature retirement.

The clearest way of becoming prepared is to have a strategy in mind. Some interviewees talked about making sure to put in the time, speaking with others to collaborate, thinking carefully about the outcome desired for each lesson, creating a plan of action, and implementing that plan while retaining flexibility. Most educators interviewed frowned upon teachers who simply "wing it." Jim Munger, the former President of the Board of Directors of the California Association of Independent Schools, says, "Flying by the seat of your pants" does not meet a passing grade for best practices.[3] Those teachers are doing a disservice to all stakeholders, including themselves. Teachers should be 100% ready before class starts. The schedule should be on the board. Everything should be setup. The teacher should not be preoccupied with grading papers. Instead, the teacher is available to answers questions and to observe student dynamics.

Another causal aspect about teacher preparedness is the effect on instructional time. In a 50-minute class, Philip Bigler, the 1998 National Teacher of the Year, believes that it truly represents about 30 minutes of pure instructional time. Therefore, time is of the essence. Once students arrive to class, some teachers say that instruction should start within two to three minutes. Philip states, "Start into what you're doing and have high expectations [of your students]." While this may sound impossible, high expectations and practicing routine behaviors have allowed many interviewees to begin instruction promptly. Several educators also alluded to treating each moment with purpose. The deliberate structure of each day must be performed with thought and care. Students know when a teacher is unprepared and is not ready to teach. It also means that this type of teacher cannot impose high expectations onto students when they, themselves, do not adhere to the same high standard.

In order to meet the needs and goals of each learner, preparation remained a common uniter for many of the educators interviewed. From a big picture perspective, Jim Munger, who also served as Head of School for a number of academic institutions, spoke about a personal education plan developed for every student at his school. Teachers, advisors, and administrators provided input to help organize and structure a plan for each student's academic and social education. Both short-term and long-term goals were penciled in, matching suitable courses to be taken with future collegiate and career aspirations in mind. On a more micro or in-classroom level, educators talked about providing multiple opportunities and ways of achieving each student's goals. This means teaching via multiple modalities to find what learning style works best. Joy Weiss, the 2010 Arizona State Teacher of the Year, states, "It can't be a one-size-fits-all education…[and] it shouldn't be a just do another worksheet [type of activity]." Meeting needs also include tapping into Multiple Intelligences Theory. A plethora of ways to demonstrate intellectual abilities must be made available for students. In all cases, preparation from the standpoint of the educator is essential in meeting the needs and helping reach the goals of students.

Lastly, imitation may be the highest form of flattery, but originality usually takes the cake. Many interviewees touched upon the topic of customization of content. Some call it, "Owning your own material." Others refer to it as, "Rewriting lessons." They both mean pretty much the same thing. In the truest sense, it is educational entrepreneurialism where a teacher creates something, whether it is a lesson or presentation, that is entirely unique and extremely efficacious in student learning. At other times, it is taking something that already exists, but making it even better, honing it to his or her specific needs and putting a personalized stamp on it. Taking the time to craft or re-craft a lesson in order to enhance student learning is all about preparedness with purpose. As Bob Feurer stated, "There is no lesson that can't be improved upon."

5. **Embrace Passion in Everything You Do**

Horace Mann, the "Father of the Common School Movement," was quoted saying, "A teacher who is attempting to teach without inspiring the pupil with a desire to learn is hammering on cold iron." Inspiration to learn comes in many forms. However, many educators interviewed believe that it is passed on by the passion of an outstanding teacher. Several interviewees recounted Teacher of the Year conferences where attendees were asked to write down the top five adjectives to describe a good teacher. In every case, passion was the most often cited attribute.

For most educators, passion is the people part of teaching. It is a genuine enjoyment of teaching and a true love of what teachers do. Quite simply, it means giving 100% of yourself every day for your students. Paul Kuhlman, the 2009 South Dakota State Teacher of the Year, states, "I don't know how to define it, but I know it when I see it. It's not just liking kids." Some teachers describe passion as the electric quality in a classroom. It is a sense of energy embodied in an educator that leads to infectious excitement with students. The passion is authentic and easily apparent to anyone observing. Pamela Harman, the 2008 Alabama State Teacher of the Year, calls teacher passion the "Secret Weapon of Teaching." She believes that students cannot help, but become interested too, if they see their teacher excited about the content. Enthusiasm can spread to kids like wildfire. It is highly contagious and most often, personality-driven.

The antipode of passionate teaching is treating the profession like a regular job. Students can tell if a teacher dislikes teaching. For instance, if a teacher states that he or she likes math, but does not really mean it, kids can figure it out. That is why faculty hiring is so important. Craig Divis, the 2010 Vermont State Teacher of the Year, comments, "A successful teacher needs to love teaching to a point where they are willing to do whatever it takes to engage their students and help them learn. Being passionate about teaching is really about motivation and dedication to your job as an educator. It is knowing that teachers have a tremendous responsibility in helping young people learn about the world, about who they are, and to realize their potential." In other words, teaching is not an 8am to 3pm occupation. It's more like 24/7. Even when a good teacher is not in the classroom, he or she is usually thinking about his or her students. Schools need to make thoughtful hiring decisions based on the above description of a successful teacher.

To make sure that passion continues to burn, some interviewees commented that it is imperative to love the subject-matter and age group taught. If that is not the case at the very onset, then sooner or later, apathy appears. Students need to see that their teacher loves teaching at the school. If not, it is impossible to expect students to show a love of learning to what is being taught. Reveta Bowers, the Head of School at the Center of Early Education, suggests making sure that there is something to look forward to every day.[4] It may be a special lesson that is planned. What are its goals? How will it work? "It might also be a student with whom you want to try connecting in a different way," says Reveta. No matter what it happens to be, having a reason to come to school excited is a good thing. Plus, it keeps passion alive in the teacher which flows down to the students.

## Final Thoughts

*Teacher Top 5* is about collaborative learning in order to elevate the level of teaching in the classroom. While the book showcases some of the best teachers in the country, everyone – no matter how new or seasoned the educator – can share their best-of-breed teaching strategies. As Roy Hudson, the 2009 Alabama State Teacher of the Year, stated, "A thousand candles can be lit from a single candle. The life of the candle will never be shortened by sharing its light." That is what *Teacher Top 5* attempts to do. In order to build a professional learning community for all stakeholders who care about education, please join us at www.teachertop5.com.

# NOTES

## Chapter 18

[1] The distance between the actual developmental level as determined by independent problem solving and the level of potential development as determined through problem solving under adult guidance, or in collaboration with more capable peers.

## Chapter 24

[2] National Commission on Teaching and America's Future (2003); Ingersoll (2003).

## Conclusion

[3] Please see www.teachertop5.com for Jim Munger's "Teacher Top 5s."

[4] Please see www.teachertop5.com for Reveta Bower's "Teacher Top 5s."